Fear not, for I have redeemed you;
I have summoned you by name; you are mine.
When you pass through the waters,
I will be with you;
and when you pass through the rivers,
they will not sweep over you.
When you walk through the fire,
you will not be burned;
the flames will not set you ablaze.
For I am the LORD, your God,
the Holy One of Israel, your Savior.

(Isaiah 43:1-3)

BE NOT AFRAID

DAVID IVASKA

InterVarsity Press
Downers Grove, Illinois

InterVarsity Press
P.O. Box 1400, Downers Grove, IL 60515
World Wide Web: www.ivpress.com
E-mail: mail@ivpress.com

InterVarsity Press® is the book-publishing division of InterVarsity Christian Fellowship/USA®, a student movement active on campus at hundreds of universities, colleges and schools of nursing in the United States of America, and a member movement of the International Fellowship of Evangelical Students. For information about local and regional activities, write Public Relations Dept., InterVarsity Christian Fellowship/USA, 6400 Schroeder Rd., P.O. Box 7895, Madison, WI 53707-7895.

Cover photograph: Zefa/Stock Market

ISBN 0-8308-1186-9

Printed in the United States of America ∞

Library of Congress Cataloging-in-Publication Data

Ivaska, David.
  Be not afraid/David Ivaska.
    p. cm.
  ISBN 0-8308-1186-9 (paper: alk. paper)
  1. Christian life—Biblical teaching. 2. Fear—Biblical teaching. 3. Bible—Textbooks. 4.
Consolation. I. Title.
  BS680.C47 I92 2000
  242'.4—dc21
                                                                          99-086865

18   17   16   15   14   13   12   11   10   9   8   7   6   5   4   3   2   1

14   13   12   11   10   09   08   07   06   05   04   03   02   01   00

Contents

Introduction

I still remember the cold, cloudy day in February when I discovered the breadth of this theme in the Bible. I was feeling overwhelmed with many unfinished tasks and perplexing situations. A sense of panic gripped me and I found myself blurting out a cry to God for help.

To my surprise, God quietly reminded me of Isaiah 43:1-2.

> Fear not, for I have redeemed you;
>> I have summoned you by name; you are mine.
> When you pass through the waters,
>> I will be with you;
> and when you pass through the rivers,
>> they will not sweep over you.
> When you walk through the fire,
>> you will not be burned;
>> the flames will not set you ablaze.

As I drank up that verse, I remembered other Isaiah "Be not afraid" passages that I had prepared for a recent spring retreat with Northwestern University's Graduate Christian Fellowship. Then, to my even deeper surprise and comfort, I thought I heard God whisper to me, "And the Bible is full of other 'Be not afraid' passages." I immediately went to look up "Do not be afraid" in the concordance. There were dozens of verses!

To help me out of my fear, I studied a different passage each day over the next several months. That daily reflection proved very healing for me. In the fall I enjoyed teaching a ten-week college class at First Presbyterian Church in Evanston entitled "Don't Panic." And then over the next summer, as part of my sabbatical study with InterVarsity Christian Fellowship, I was asked by my pastor, David Handley, to write a daily personal and weekly small group study guide to parallel his sermon series, "Do Not Be Afraid." I put together a guide with the help of my wife, Sally, and our friend Holly Hudnut Halliday.

Throughout this time many friends had shared with me how helpful such a study would be for them, so I've created this guide for wider distribution. I'm grateful for their encouragement! And I'm thankful for Sally, who during my periodic states of panic has insightfully reminded me to take to heart these discoveries about God's promises.

Many Facets of Fear

The Bible does not dismiss people facing fear. Instead, God comes again and again to those challenged or discouraged by fear.

There is an alarming number of angles from which fear can ambush us. When and where we least suspect it, fear takes hold of us—sometimes for a fleeting moment, other times for a paralyzing length of time. In Scripture we can find almost any type of fear we might face (both external and internal): fear resulting from adventure as well as tragedy; fear of launching a new effort or finishing a never-ending task; fear associated with leadership and responsibility; fear of abandonment and rejection; fear of insecurity and inadequacy; fear of failure and living in vain; fear of feeling stuck with no way out and things going from bad to worse; fear of sickness, death or loss of a loved one; fear of ridicule and revenge; fear of sharing our faith and being stretched in our faith—and the list could go on!

False Assurance, Real Hope

Often when we want to comfort someone who is afraid we say, "Do not be afraid, everything will be okay." Unfortunately, things are not always okay; in fact, they often get worse. And that is when fear is particularly gripping! The Bible takes a strikingly different approach; it also says "Do not be afraid," but adds "because our God comes" (Isaiah 35:3-4; 40:9). What a critical difference! Far better than being told we will not face troubles (a false hope) is being given an inner strength to face those troubles (an enduring hope).

What God can bring into fearful hearts and situations is the key to not being afraid. Paul had it right when he urged the Philippians to "not be anxious about anything, but by prayer and petition, with thanksgiving, present your requests to God. And the peace of God, which transcends all understanding, will guard your hearts and minds in Christ Jesus" (Philippians 4:6-7) The writer of Hebrews reminds us, "God has said, 'Never will I leave you; never will I forsake you'" (Hebrews 13:5).

God Wants to Deliver Us from Fear

In looking ahead to the coming of Jesus, Zechariah, the father of John the Baptist, declares, "He has raised up a horn of salvation for us in the house of his servant David . . . to rescue us from the hand of our enemies, and to enable us to serve him without fear in holiness and righeousness before him all our days" (Luke 1:69-75). King David recognized that God wants to free us to serve him without fear when he said, "I sought the LORD, and he answered me; he delivered me from all my fears" (Psalm 34:4). And the apostle Paul encourages Timothy by reminding him, "For God has not given us a spirit of timidity, but a spirit of power, of love and of self-discipline" (2 Timothy 1:7).

The key, however, to not being afraid is learning to fear God. Again in Psalm 34 David declares,

"This poor man called, and the LORD heard him,
he saved him out of all his troubles.
The angel of the LORD encamps around those *who fear him,*

and he delivers them.

Taste and see that the LORD is good;
blessed is the man who takes refuge in him.
Fear the LORD, you his saints,
for those *who fear him* lack nothing. . . .

Come, my children, listen to me;
I will teach you *the fear of the LORD.*" (author's italics)

I suspect that too often we fear circumstances, rather than the Lord of those situations. Or we expect God to remove fear from us without any move on our part to fear the God who made us or redeemed us and to understand and trust his ways.

Getting the Most Out of These Studies

If you have never read through the whole Bible, these "Be not afraid" passages will take you from beginning to end, introducing you to many major Bible characters and events. The study starts with Adam and Eve's fear of facing God after disobeying him and ends with the church's longing for trials and tribulations to end. God searches for Adam and Eve, who are hiding in the garden, and does not give up that search for men and women until the very end of this world when he restores his people and places them in a new garden where there is no more fear. Thanks be to God!

Let me invite you to use this study guide in several ways:

Set aside 10-15 minutes a day to reflect on one day's reading. Each day the introductions, questions and prayer will help you reflect on what the passage says, what it means and what it means for you today. Set aside a place and time that will facilitate a regular meeting with God.

Participate in a small group Bible study and use the group studies included at the end of each week's readings. This will help you care and pray for each other as you face any number of fears. God's Word used by God's Spirit in the context of God's community is a threefold bond that will serve you well.

Use the "Weekly Wrap-up" questions at the end of each group study—either on your own or with a group—to review and summarize what you are learning from the daily studies each week.

Use this guide in family devotions or to prepare for sermons or talks. Note that some weeks can easily stand alone. For example, week nine introduces the seven "be not afraids" of Easter. Week eight covers the "be not afraids" of Christmas. Week two focuses on fear in leadership.

Be on the lookout for friends at work or school, in your neighborhood or church, from your past or in your family who may be facing fear. Encourage them out of what you are learning. Give them copies to study for themselves.

Keep in mind that what you learn could be of use to you in the future. You may not be facing a particular fear now; thank God for that. But be alert; part of fear's strength is in its surprise. Your strength lies in knowing the God of peace who says, "*When* you pass through the waters I will be with you" (Isaiah 43:2, author's italic). Store up God's Word in your heart now for the Spirit to retrieve when needed.

May this study encourage and strengthen you as it has me on many occasions since that dreadful morning in February.

David Ivaska

Week One

From Fear to Faith

*Genesis Introduces Us
to God's Reassuring Word of Hope*

DAY ONE

Hiding from God: Adam

The man [Adam] and his wife [Eve] heard the sound of the LORD God as he was walking in the garden in the cool of the day, and they hid from the LORD God among the trees of the garden. But the LORD God called to the man, "Where are you?"

He answered, "I heard you in the garden, and I was afraid because I was naked; so I hid." (Genesis 3:8-10; see also Genesis 3:1-7, 21-24)

What do you do when you feel afraid? How do you think God responds to your fear? Adam's reaction in these verses is the first experience of fear recorded in the Bible. Here we also discover a striking response on God's part—he searches for Adam. Again and again in Scripture we will see how God seeks out those he

NORWEGIAN BAY BOOKS & GIFTS
W2511 HWY 23
GREEN LAKE, WI 54941
(920)294-7394

1 0830811869
   BE NOT AFRAID   6.99
                       Sub Total   6.99
                       Sales Tax   .38
                       Total Due   7.37
                              MC   7.37

This Transaction # 2006750
NOV 2, 2001 15:34 2 -

loves when they are afraid. God seeks us out as well.

Why does fear cause us to hide?

What do you learn about God as you see him looking for Adam and Eve when they were afraid?

What fear are you hiding, or what fear is causing you to hide from God or others?

Imagine going for a walk with God in a nearby garden. How would you describe your fears to God?

Concerned Creator, what a relief to know that you are eager to hear my fears, to clothe me and even more to restore to me all the fullness of peace and joy that you intended for me from the very day of creation! May my fear not turn me from you but toward you.

DAY TWO

Facing Tragedy: Hagar

God heard the boy crying, and the angel of God called to Hagar from heaven and said to her, "What is the matter, Hagar? Do not be afraid; God has heard the boy crying as he lies there. Lift the boy up and take him by the hand, for I will make him a great nation."

*Then God opened her eyes and she saw a well of water. . . . God was
with the boy as he grew up. (Genesis 21:17-21; see also Genesis 21:8-16)*

Experiencing fear is always unpleasant. But the fear brought on by
rejection and tragedy is particularly painful. No matter who we
are we can be encouraged by this story of how God answered a
baby's cry and a mother's despair.

Hagar was a slave woman working away from home. She had been
told that her son was not the son who would inherit God's promised blessing. Then she had been sent away by Abraham, who
fathered her son, Ishmael, and by his wife, Sarah. Hagar was
stranded in the desert listening to the cries of her hungry, thirsty and
dying son. What words and phrases would you use to describe her
fear?

What do we learn about God's love and intentions in this story?

How could the story of God's care for Hagar encourage you or
someone you know?

*Thank you, God, that you are not hard of hearing and that you
come close to those whose pain is too great to bear. Encourage me
to lift up the crying as you did with Hagar. Open my eyes to see
your provision of thirst-quenching wells of water.*

DAY THREE

Much to Fear: Isaac

That night the LORD *appeared to him [Isaac] and said, "I am the God of your father Abraham. Do not be afraid, for I am with you; I will bless you and will increase the number of your descendants for the sake of my servant Abraham." (Genesis 26:24; see also Genesis 26:1-33)*

Fear can bombard us from any side, even many sides. Isaac knew that only too well. In chapter 26 alone, Isaac faces a famine (vv. 1-6), a threat to his life (vv. 7-11), a conflict over water rights (vv. 12-22) and a family feud (vv. 19-34). At the height of conflict from many sides, Isaac hears a word of blessing that gets passed from one generation to another.

Notice that God does not allay Isaac's fears by telling him everything will be all right. In light of that, what is the significance of God's statement to Isaac: "Do not be afraid, for I am with you"?

What is the significance of "I will bless you"?

What is the significance of "I will increase your descendants for the sake of my servant Abraham"?

In what situations do you feel overwhelmed, and what fear does that generate or intensify in you?

How does knowing that God is on your side encourage you?

God of both Abraham and Isaac, thank you that your assurances extend from one generation to another, covering any fears I may have for myself, for my parents and for future generations.

DAY FOUR

Two Conflicting Desires: Jacob

"I am God, the God of your father," he said. "Do not be afraid to go down to Egypt, for I will make you into a great nation there. I will go down to Egypt with you, and I will surely bring you back again. And Joseph's own hand will close your eyes." (Genesis 46:3-4; see also Genesis 45:25—46:7)

Jacob had already experienced great sacrifice and loss, not the least of which was thinking he had lost Joseph, his youngest and favorite son. But he also had come to know—through a great deal of wrestling with God—God's promise to bless him and make him a great nation. At the end of his life he hears the stunning news that his son is ruling in Egypt. Yes, he would go to see his son, but how would God make him a great nation in Egypt?

When you are forced to make unexpected and often conflicting choices that pit strong desires against each other, what fears arise?

How does God's answer help Jacob to believe that both of his passions—seeing his son alive and seeing God build a new nation—could be realized in this strange turn of events?

When have you been caught in the bind of choosing between two strong desires?

What did you fear losing in such a choice?

How did God open a new, though possibly risky or surprising, way forward?

Thank you, God, that you are not restricted to our limited choices but often have in store for us surprising new ways to satisfy our deepest desires and your great purposes.

DAY FIVE

Deserving Retribution: Joseph's Brothers

His brothers then came and threw themselves down before him. "We are your slaves," they said.

But Joseph said to them, "Don't be afraid. Am I in the place of God? You intended to harm me, but God intended it for good to accomplish what is now being done, the saving of many lives." (Genesis 50:18-20; see also Genesis 49:29—50:17)

Have you ever been afraid of some punishment you knew you totally deserved? Joseph's brothers found themselves facing that kind of fear. Decades earlier, out of bitter jealousy for Joseph's favored status with their father, his brothers sold him into slavery. Joseph ended up in Egypt and became a wise ruler. During a severe famine, all the world came begging him for food—including his own brothers.

How is Joseph's response to his brothers both stunning and wise?

_____

Think of someone who might fear interacting with you because they know they have wronged you somehow. How might you pattern your response after Joseph's?

_____

Think of a situation in which you fear getting what you could deserve. How might Joseph's story give you strength to approach the person you have wronged?

Holy God, I deserve all the punishment for my sins that you could exact. But, merciful God, would you forgive me and turn my wrong intentions into your redeeming acts? I will be your grateful servant.

DAY SIX

_____

Facing Death: Joseph

"Don't be afraid. . . ." Joseph said to his brothers, "I am about to die. But God will surely come to your aid and take you up out of this land to the land he promised on oath to Abraham, Isaac and Jacob." (Genesis 50:21, 24; see also Genesis 50:15-26)

Have you ever been with someone who is close to death or in great difficulty, and they prove to be more encouraging to you than you are to them? That was true with Joseph and his family.

Describe Joseph's state of mind as he approached his death.

What enables someone at the end of his or her life, or in the midst of great difficulty, to have the strength to encourage others rather than be the one needing encouragement?

Who has surprised you with their words of encouragement when you would have thought that they were themselves needing encouragement?

God of Abraham, Isaac and Jacob, thank you for building into Joseph this deep conviction that you would surely come to his family's aid and bring them into the promised land. Work in my life that with my last breath I too may encourage others with the same kind of confidence that you will take us home as you said you would.

Small Group Study

God's Reassuring Word of Hope

The Bible's very first statement of "Do not be afraid" is worth special attention. In particular we see the struggle Abram has in embracing it. Even after being told by God not to be afraid, Abram has serious questions that need answers before he can move from fear to faith. How true that is for each of us! *Read Genesis 15:1-21.*

Do Not Be Afraid (v. 1)

1. Imagine you are Abram. Chapters 11—14 tell us that he is a recent immigrant who is fleeing famine. His family is feuding over wealth. A family member has been captured in regional fighting and needs rescuing. God promised Abram that he would become the father of many nations, yet at eighty he still has no children. What fears might you be facing?

2. In the midst of those fears, what encouragement would you gain from God speaking to your fear before you even expressed it?

How would it help to have God call you by name?

describe himself as your shield?

describe himself as your great reward?

3. What growing fear do you have that something great will actually never work out?

From what do you need shielding?

What Can You Give Me? (vv. 2-7)

4. In spite of God's reassuring words in verse 1, Abram wants to know what God will give him. What is God's threefold response?

5. How could God's response move Abram from fear to faith?

6. In what situation have reassuring words (from God or friends) not quieted your fears?

7. How does this incident with Abram give you a hint of hope?

But How Can I Know? (vv. 8-21)

8. Again, in spite of God's reassuring words in verses 2-7, Abram struggles with how he can know all of this for sure. What surprising answers does God give him (vv. 13-16)?

9. How would God's prediction of things getting worse before they get better help to answer his dilemma?

10. How does Christ's sacrifice on the cross parallel this situation?

How does it help to settle the question "How can we know for sure that we will inherit all of God's promises for us?"

Weekly Wrap-Up

What range of fears did the daily studies in Genesis introduce?

What perspective on quieting our fears does each of the "Do not be afraid" passages add?

Week Two

Be Strong & Courageous

Moses, Joshua & Gideon
on the Challenge of Leading Others

- -

DAY ONE

Anticipating the Worst: Moses

When you go to war against your enemies and see horses and chariots and an army greater than yours, do not be afraid of them, because the LORD your God, who brought you up out of Egypt, will be with you. . . . The priest shall come forward and address the army. . . . "Do not be faint-hearted or afraid; do not be terrified or give way to panic before them. For the LORD your God is the one who goes with you to fight for you against your enemies to give you victory." (Deuteronomy 20:1-4)

It is one thing to run into trouble in the course of a day. But what about those days when, before you even begin, you know you are going to face odds that are definitely against you and you will need to take a very unpopular course of action? What do you do? God's instructions to Moses regarding how to anticipate those fearful, dreadful wars can guide us as well.

___

In what ways does having time to think about a fearful situation only increase your fear?

___

How did God anticipate those feelings here when he said, "Do not be terrified or give way to panic"?

___

What past, present and future assurance does God give Moses?

___

How would each of those assurances help to diminish the fear Moses and the people are anticipating?

___

What do you dread the most this week or next?

___

What difference would it make to know that God will fight for you, as he has in the past, until you see victory?

All-knowing and unflappable God, you know I often think the worst when I anticipate a fearful situation. Change my attitude by reminding me that you go before me and fight beside me.

DAY TWO

Facing a New & Daunting Task: Joshua

Do not let this Book of the Law depart from your mouth; meditate on it day and night, so that you may be careful to do everything written in it. Then you will be prosperous and successful. Have I not commanded you? Be strong and courageous. Do not be terrified; do not be discouraged, for the LORD your God is with you wherever you go. (Joshua 1:8-9; see also Joshua 1:1-10)

As I was with Moses, so I will be with you. (Joshua 1:5)

Moses was an unbelievably strong leader. But now he is gone from the scene. It is up to Joshua not only to fill Moses' sandals but to move a million people from wandering in the wilderness to claiming the Promised Land.

What questions might come to Joshua's mind in succeeding Moses?

What real or imaginary fears might he face with this new and daunting task?

How does God counter Joshua's fears?

How would daily insights into God's Word make up for the loss of his predecessor?

What new and daunting task are you facing this year?

_____

What new resolution could you make to ensure you take time daily to meditate on God's Word?

_____

What new strength would that bring to your leadership in your various areas of responsibility this year?

_____

Author of all life and leadership, inspire me each day to face new and daunting tasks through the insight and wisdom of your Word.

DAY THREE

_____

Dealing with Sin: Joshua

Do not be afraid, do not be discouraged. Take the whole army with you and go up and attack Ai. For I have delivered into your hands the king of Ai, his people, his city and his land. (Joshua 8:1; see also Joshua 7:1— 8:12)

_____

Israel had experienced a major victory with the battle of Jericho, but Achan, against very clear instructions from God, secretly stole some of the valuables left over from that battle. Full of confidence from the victory at Jericho, Israel then attempted to capture a little village called Ai but was soundly defeated—simply because of Achan's sin. Now that sin has been dealt with, they are questioning how to proceed. These are God's words of encouragement to try again.

Why was it so important for God to step forward as he did and assure Joshua that, in spite of this failure, he should take courage and move on to the battles that await him?

When have you been afraid to move forward because of something you did wrong?

How could you renew your courage to move ahead?

Father, I wonder if my sin, even sin already confessed, makes me unworthy to push on with a new assignment. Remind me that with your forgiveness also comes a renewal of spirit to walk in newness of life and in the strength of your might.

DAY FOUR

Failing to Seek God: Joshua

The LORD said to Joshua, "Do not be afraid of them; I have given them into your hand. Not one of them will be able to withstand you."
The sun stopped in the middle of the sky and delayed going down about a full day. There has never been a day like it before or since, a day when the LORD listened to a man. Surely the LORD was fighting for Israel! (Joshua 10:8, 13-14; see also Joshua 10:1-15)

Following on the heels of the failure that resulted from Achan's wrongdoing is the failure to do what is right. Sometimes that can be just as disastrous, as Joshua found out with Gibeon in this passage. Joshua was under clear orders to destroy every tribe in Canaan because of their extreme corruption. But people from one of the conquered cities tricked Joshua by dressing up like starving travelers from a far-off land and persuaded him to make a peace treaty with them. Instead of praying about it first, Joshua simply agreed, only to discover that he had been tricked.

When you fail to do something that is critical like Joshua did and you then have to live with whatever consequences that failure brings on, what fears creep into your mind?

What do you learn about God from his encouragement to Joshua to push on in spite of Joshua's failure to seek him?

What do you learn about God from the way that he causes the sun to stand still so that Joshua can finish his task?

At times we all fail at doing what we know we should do. In your own life, where do you fail in doing what is right?

What would it mean to you for God to say to you, "Do not be afraid, let's push on; I'll help you finish what's important before the day ends"?

Thanks be to God who rescues us from this struggle of doing what we should not do and not doing what we should do.

DAY FIVE

Facing an Unfinished Task: Joshua

The LORD said to Joshua, "Do not be afraid of them, because by this time tomorrow I will hand all of them over to Israel, slain." . . .
As the LORD commanded his servant Moses, so Moses commanded Joshua, and Joshua did it; he left nothing undone of all that the LORD commanded Moses. (Joshua 11:6, 15; see also Joshua 11:1-23)

A s we come to the end of Joshua's life, we read about his fear of wrapping up a mission. Over a dozen kings from the north, south, east and west had joined forces to try and stop him from completing his mission. Then once their enemies were defeated, he had to divide all the land among the twelve tribes of Israel.

What fears often surround the completion of a major task?

In what ways does God show that he is equal to this unfinished task facing Joshua?

What vested interest would God have in Joshua completing this mission?

What job is hanging over your head?

To what extent do you believe your God is big enough to see you through to the completion of that task?

God, you are the Alpha and Omega, the Beginning and the End. You have shown yourself faithful to Joshua to the very end of his mission and you have promised that you would not rest until we find our rest in you. Give me courage to finish whatever job I need to finish and to believe that you are bigger than any task I face.

DAY SIX

When Timidity & Uncertainty Immobilize: Gideon

But the LORD said to him, "Peace! Do not be afraid. You are not going to die."
So Gideon built an altar to the LORD there and called it The LORD is Peace. (Judges 6:23-24; see also Judges 6:1-40)

The story of Gideon is a series of encounters with God that reveal one uncertainty after another. When we first meet Gideon, he is forced to harvest in secret because of the threat of the Midianites. When an angel appears saying, "The LORD is with you, mighty warrior!" (Judges 6:12), Gideon asks why he is having so much trouble. When God commissions Gideon to go and defeat Midian, Gideon again questions how he could do that since he is in the weakest clan of Israel. God assures Gideon of his presence, Gideon demands a sign that proves God is speaking. A sign is given, but when God gives him his first assignment, Gideon decides to only work in the middle of the night when no one can see him. Finally on the eve of his major assignment Gideon puts out the fleece (his sign), not just once but twice, to make *sure* that God is going to use him to defeat Midian.

What fears does Gideon seem to be wrestling with in these different encounters?

Why do so many of our fears have the power to immobilize us?

What encouragement do you gain from seeing how God very patiently answers each one of Gideon's questions?

Where in your life do you need to see the Lord of peace appear?

Sovereign Lord, you are first called Lord of Peace with Gideon. Be that to me today!

Small Group Study

Nowhere to Turn

The message "Do not be afraid" in the Bible, more often than not, comes to leaders being called upon to lead in a situation, whether they see themselves as leaders or not. Fear crouches at the door of every leader, often making huge demands on the choices and risks a leader entertains. Yet fear is often the context in which leadership is displayed most significantly. Throughout the Bible we see that God is fully aware of both of those realities.

God does not shrink back from fearful situations and even calls us to step forward and display God-empowered strength and courage. At the same time God knows our every thought and seems constantly aware of the fears we face before, during and after a major undertaking. As we are led by God in the midst of fear, we will lead more strongly whether we are at home, work, school or church. *Read Exodus 14:1—15:6.*

The Complaint—Who Is in Charge Here? (14:1-12)

1. The expressions "between a rock and a hard place," "up against the wall" and "nowhere to turn" aptly describe the predicament Israel is in with the Red Sea on one side and Pharaoh's approaching army on the other. Yes, God had just delivered Israel out of Egypt, but now they face a major setback. What fears does such a situation provoke?

What crisis in leadership does it create?

2. Why is complaining about leadership often the first response in fearful situations?

when facing setbacks?

3. When have you been tempted to complain first in a fearful situation? (Describe your fear and the crisis in leadership.)

The Challenge—Look for God to Be in Charge! (14:13-29)

4. What does Moses see or believe—that the people do not see— that allows him to call on the people not to be afraid but to stand firm (14:1-4, 13-14)?

5. Why is it important for a leader to see fear as a *context* for leadership rather than a *crisis* in leadership?

Why would it be even more important to see fear not as a *limitation* of human resources but as an *opportunity* for divine resources?

6. What different concerns of Israel's does God address in providing deliverance? (Look at vv. 15-18, 19-20, 21-22, 23-28.)

What assurance does that give you when your back is up against the wall?

The Chorus—I Sing the Mighty Power of God (14:29—15:6)

7. What reversal does God's activity produce in the people's hearts and minds?

8. When have you been impressed by God's deliverance?

9. Moses sang a song as a tribute to God's deliverance. How could you celebrate what God has done in your life?

Weekly Wrap-Up

What fears did Moses, Joshua and Gideon face?

What crisis in leadership did each provoke?

How was each situation a context for leadership and an opportunity for God's power?

What change in perspective did each "Do not be afraid" bring?

Week Three

If Only You Could See

Elisha to Daniel & God's Invitation
to See the Impossible

- -

DAY ONE

No More to Give: Elijah

Elijah said to her, "Don't be afraid. . . . The God of Israel says: 'The jar of flour will not be used up and the jug of oil will not run dry until the day of the LORD gives rain on the land.'" (1 Kings 17:13-14; see also 1 Kings 17:7-24)

Compelled to give your last. That is what this widow was being asked to do. Israel was in the midst of a severe drought and the prophet Elijah was asked by God to go and live with this widow from neighboring Zarephath. Unfortunately, the widow was hardly in a position to give Elijah the food he asked for because she was preparing to feed her only son one last meager meal before facing starvation.

Jesus himself points to this story as an unequaled model of faith

(Luke 4:24-30). What faith did both Elijah and the widow display in this dire situation?

What fears bombard us when we are asked to give our very last?

What does faith call on us to believe about God in difficult situations?

When have you seen God give you, day after day, just what you needed, even though you thought you had nothing more to give?

Father, give me this day my daily bread and the faith of this widow to believe that you can give when I have no more to give.

DAY TWO

Seeing the Unseen: Elisha

When the servant of the man of God got up and went out early the next morning, an army with horses and chariots had surrounded the city. "Oh, my lord, what shall we do?" the servant asked.

"Don't be afraid," the prophet answered. "Those who are with us are more than those who are with them."

And Elisha prayed, "O LORD, open his eyes so he may see." Then the Lord opened the servant's eyes, and he looked and saw the hills full of horses and chariots of fire all around Elisha. (2 Kings 6:15-17; see also 2 Kings 6:8-23)

Often when we face very challenging situations, we only look at the resources we have at hand or the possibilities we see available. Like Elisha's servant, we then panic and wonder what to do. But faith sees what cannot be seen, as Elisha so powerfully displays. Faith supplies new resources and possibilities.

Why is it so frightening at times to be limited to our own resources or options?

Elisha could have simply told his servant not to worry, things would be okay. Instead, why did he pray and ask God to open the servant's eyes to see what cannot be seen?

In what situations do limited resources or options make you wonder where you can turn next?

Who would you ask to pray with you that your eyes would be open to see God's resources available to you? (Or, who needs you to pray with them?)

I pray that the eyes of my heart may be enlightened in order that I may know the hope to which I have been called, the riches of my glorious inheritance, and the incomparably great power in me as I believe. (Adapted from Paul's prayer in Ephesians 1:18-19.)

DAY THREE

The Battle Is the Lord's: Jehoshaphat

Listen, King Jehoshaphat and all who live in Judah and Jerusalem! This is what the LORD says to you: "Do not be afraid or discouraged because of this vast army. For the battle is not yours, but God's." (2 Chronicles 20:15; see also 2 Chronicles 20:1-30)

Sometimes fear is so gripping that all we can do is resign ourselves to God's mercy. Jehoshaphat and the people had no idea whether or not God would deliver them from the enemies bearing down on them. But they had called a fast and were saying to God that no matter what they would continue to stand in the temple and cry out to him in their distress: "We do not know what to do, but our eyes are upon you" (20:12).

What kind of fear provokes this kind of resignation to God's mercy?

What difference does it make to know that in those situations God steps forward to say that the battle is not ours but his?

What battles are you fighting these days that really are not yours but God's?

How would a change of perspective about these battles affect your fears?

Forgive me, Lord, for those times that I am slow to let go of battles that are not really mine but yours. Teach me to stand firm—and even to fast as Jehoshaphat did—and say, "I do not know what to do, but my eyes are upon you"!

DAY FOUR

Gaining Confidence: Jeremiah

"Ah, Sovereign LORD," I [Jeremiah] said, "I do not know how to speak; I am only a child."
    But the LORD said to me, "Do not say, 'I am only a child.' You must go to everyone I send you to and say whatever I command you. Do not be afraid of them, for I am with you and will rescue you," declares the Lord.
    Get yourself ready! Stand up and say to them whatever I command you. Do not be terrified by them. . . . They will fight against you but will not overcome you, for I am with you and will rescue you. (Jeremiah 1:6-7, 17, 19; see also Jeremiah 6:1-19)

Feelings of inadequacy can often be our undoing, stirring up tre-mendous fear in us—often very unrealistic fears. This can be par-ticularly acute in situations that we have never faced before. In the prophet Jeremiah's case God gave him the very difficult task of breaking the news to Judah that God had reached his limit with them and he was sending them into captivity. And even though God would bring them back after seventy years, Judah would reject this last messenger.

Why are feelings of inadequacy and fear so easily intertwined?

What sense of adequacy would Jeremiah find when God responds to his fear the way he does?

How would God's words bring a calming effect?

How do God's words give Jeremiah courage to speak out?

In what capacity do you feel most inadequate?

What sense of adequacy, calm or strength can you gain from knowing God is present with you?

Though I may feel inadequate to do what you call me to do, may your adequacy calm and strengthen me.

DAY FIVE

Bold to Speak Out: Ezekiel

The people to whom I am sending you are obstinate and stubborn. Say to them, "This is what the Sovereign LORD says." And whether they listen or fail to listen—for they are a rebellious house—they will know that a prophet has been among them. And you, son of man, do not be afraid of them or their words. Do not be afraid, though briers and thorns are all around you and you live among scorpions. . . . You must speak my words to them, whether they listen or fail to listen, for they are rebellious. But you, son of man, listen to what I say to you. (Ezekiel 2:4-8; see also Ezekiel 2:9-15)

Some jobs are inherently risky and unpopular. And with such tasks comes plenty of opportunity to be afraid, to give up altogether and to say that it is not worth it anymore to do what is being asked. God knew that he was asking Ezekiel to complete a difficult assignment. But God also came to say, "Do not be afraid. Speak out."

What makes Ezekiel's assignment such a challenging one?

What fears might be involved?

One of Jesus' most common names is *Son of Man* (after Ezekiel). What encouragement does it give you to know that Jesus himself took great risks to do what he did for us, even though thorns were all around him, even at death?

What risky or unpopular stand are you being urged to take?

In what way has it been good for you to hear the challenge not to be afraid and speak out?

Lord Jesus, Son of Man, thank you for not shrinking back in giving

*yourself to me, in spite of all sorts of opposition. As you did with
Ezekiel, help me to persist though briars and thorns surround me.*

DAY SIX

A Perplexing Future &
Unanswered Prayer: Daniel

*I was left alone, gazing at this great vision; I had no strength left, my face
turned deathly pale and I was helpless. Then I heard him speaking. . . .
A hand touched me and set me trembling on my hands and knees.
"Do not be afraid, Daniel. Since the first day that you set your mind to
gain understanding and to humble yourself before your God, your prayers
were heard, and I have come in response to them. But the prince of the
Persian kingdom resisted me for twenty-one days. . . . I was detained. . . .
Now I have come to explain to you what will happen to your people in the
future. . . .
"Do not be afraid, O man highly esteemed," he said. "Peace! Be strong."
(Daniel 10:8, 10, 12-13, 19; see also Daniel 10:1-18)*

Unanswered prayer. A confusing future. These realities take an
emotional toll on us. They did for the prophet Daniel. But
Daniel learned a surprising lesson in the process.

What fears are triggered by ominous predictions about the future,
as well as unanswered prayers?

Though the angel who was commissioned to answer Daniel's
prayer and explain a fearful vision of the future was delayed for
three weeks because of some heavenly battle going on, he eventu-

ally broke through. What fresh insight do you gain from this expla-
nation of the delay?

What long-standing unanswered prayer do you have, and what
emotional toll has it begun to take in your life?

What change in perspective might you have knowing that God may
be eager to answer that prayer but may be delayed by Satan or circumstances before he breaks through?

*O Lord, help me to remember that we are wrestling not against
flesh and blood but against the spiritual forces of evil in heavenly
places. May this deepen my urgency to pray even more, to not lose
heart with prayers that are not immediately answered and to wait
for your strong right arm of eventual deliverance.*

Small Group Study

God's Invitation to See the Impossible

It may be hard to know whether losing perspective causes fear or
fear causes one to lose perspective. In either case, losing perspective is very unsettling. And the circumstance that we are in all of a
sudden becomes much larger than any resource available to us.
The mark of a godly person is the ability to see what God sees in a
situation and what he brings to it. *Read 2 Kings 18:17—19:22.*

On What Are You Basing Your Confidence? (18:17—19:4)

1. In what different ways did Sennacherib's letter try to undermine the peoples' confidence?

2. What fear would his ridicule, boasting and month's siege provoke?

3. How do ridicule, boasting, comparison and constant pressure magnify any already existing fear?

4. When have these intensified your own fear?

a friend's fear?

Don't Be Afraid of What You Have Heard (19:5-19; see parallel story in 2 Chronicles 32:6-8)

5. How does Hezekiah encourage the people not to fear and not to be overwhelmed by the ridicule and boasting?

6. How have you come to know that God is greater than any fear you have had to face?

7. Note what happens after Hezekiah encourages the people. What fear is expressed in 19:14-19?

8. Why might someone struggle with fear even though he or she is able to tell others not to be afraid?

When have you experienced that yourself?

9. Note how Hezekiah lays out his fear before the Lord (19:14). What strength comes from doing that?

You Have Really Insulted God (19:20-22)

10. Note how God himself absorbs Sennacherib's ridicule and boasting (19:22). What strength comes from knowing that God takes all that on himself?

11. Think of a situation in which someone's words really devastated you. Ask God to step in the way of that word and absorb the blow for you. Take time as a group (perhaps in pairs) to encourage each other like Hezekiah did and to "lay before the Lord" your fears.

Weekly Wrap-Up

What various disappointments or difficulties undermined the confidence of this week's Old Testament characters?

Why are these so devastating at times?

What different reasons does God give not to be afraid?

How would these perspectives be so helpful?

What account did you value or identify with the most and why?

Week Four

Encouraging Others Who Fear

How Others Brought God's Word of Hope to Those in Need

- -

DAY ONE

Offering Protection: David & Abiathar

Abiathar, a son of Ahimelech son of Ahitub, escaped and fled to join David. He told David that Saul had killed the priests of the LORD. Then David said to Abiathar . . . "I am responsible for the death of your father's whole family. Stay with me; don't be afraid; the man who is seeking your life is seeking mine also. You will be safe with me." (1 Samuel 22:20-23; see also 1 Samuel 21:1-9; 22:6-23)

W hat an agonizing situation for David to hear this report of eighty-five priests slaughtered including Abiathar's father. Just days before Ahitub had helped David escape Saul's pursuing army.

It is one thing to tell someone, "Don't be afraid, things will be okay," and yet quite another to say, "Here, stay with me, don't be afraid. We are in this together and you will be safe with me." In what ways are those two statements profoundly different?

How would David's words encourage Abiathar?

Has someone recently come to you for help? Think about how you tried to encourage them and compare your words of encouragement with those of David.

Father of compassion and God of all comfort, may I comfort those in trouble with the same comfort with which you have comforted me. Help me to love others not in word only but also in deed. And if I have caused anyone undue harm, help me to have courage to accept that responsibility and take steps to doubly care for them.

DAY TWO

Encouraging Perseverance: Jonathan & David

While David was at Horesh in the Desert of Ziph, he learned that Saul had come out to take his life. And Saul's son Jonathan went to David at Horesh and helped him find strength in God. "Don't be afraid," he said. "My father Saul will not lay a hand on you. You will be king over Israel, and I will be second to you. Even my father Saul knows this." The two of them made a covenant before the Lord. (1 Samuel 23:15-18; see also 1 Samuel 23:7-14, 19-22; 24:9-11)

F ear is often very short-sighted. We only see the crisis staring us in the face at the moment. We very easily lose perspective. A strong characteristic of encouragement is helping someone to see the long view. This is exactly what Jonathan did for his friend David when he was deeply distressed.

In this passage King Saul (the father of David's friend Jonathan) is pursuing David's 600 men with 3,000 soldiers, out of jealousy and rage. David has been forced to flea to the country of the Philistines—bitter enemies of Israel. In fact, at this time the Philistines are attacking David's only allied village. Even the village is prepared to turn David over to Saul. David cannot stay in the same place more than one night. The only safe place is a desert cave.

What risks does Jonathan take in going out to help David?

Reflect on Jonathan's words of encouragement to David and the significance of his intention, reminder, information and covenant. What friend can you think of who has lost perspective?

How could you follow Jonathan's example of friendship?

Thank you Jesus that you made me your friend and that you will stick with me to the very end, constantly reminding me of your precious and very great promises. Help me not to lose sight of this, both for myself and for others.

DAY THREE

Keeping Promises: David & Mephibosheth

David asked, "Is there anyone still left of the house of Saul to whom I can show kindness for Jonathan's sake?"

Now there was a servant of Saul's household named Ziba. They called him to appear before David. . . .

Ziba answered the king, "There is still a son of Jonathan; he is crippled in both feet." . . .

When Mephibosheth son of Jonathan, the son of Saul, came to David, he bowed down to pay him honor. . . .

"Don't be afraid," David said to him, "for I will surely show you kindness for the sake of your father Jonathan. I will restore to you all the land that belonged to your grandfather Saul and you will always eat at my table."

Mephibosheth bowed down and said, "What is your servant that you should notice a dead dog like me?" (2 Samuel 9:1-3, 6-8; see also 2 Samuel 9:1-13)

Saul had tortuously pursued David, forcing him to run for his life. Now, all but one of Saul's family had been killed, including David's best friend. No one would have ever noticed if King David had not kept his promise to be kind to Saul's family.

What impresses you about David's actions? Why?

What convictions go into keeping promises and showing kindness?

Who could you keep a promise or show kindness to?

Who better to come to than you, God, for help in this area! For you alone are matchless in making and keeping your promises and showing us unending kindness. May I live up to your name.

DAY FOUR

Providing for Needs: David & Solomon

David also said to Solomon his son, "Be strong and courageous, and do the work. Do not be afraid or discouraged, for the LORD God, my God, is with you. He will not fail you or forsake you until all the work for the service of the temple of the LORD is finished. The divisions of the priests and Levites are ready for all the work on the temple of God, and every willing man skilled in any craft will help you in all the work." (1 Chronicles 28:20-21; see also 1 Chronicles 28:1-19)

When someone young and inexperienced is given a huge task, offering to help with the job is encouraging to them. At the end of his life, David commissioned his young son Solomon to build the temple. David made it very clear that everything Solomon would need to do the job was already provided. What better start for a young leader?

List all the reminders of provision David gives his son.

How is this kind of support structure critical in diminishing fear?

What did it cost David to make these kinds of provisions available to Solomon?

What potential young leader could you encourage either in your family or work?

What provisions does that person need to be free from fear?

God, our Provider, I praise you that everything I need for life and godliness you provide for me through your son Jesus Christ. May I reflect that spirit to others.

DAY FIVE

"God Is Greater": Hezekiah & His Officers

[Hezekiah] appointed military officers over the people and assembled them before him in the square at the city gate and encouraged them with these words: "Be strong and courageous. Do not be afraid or discouraged because of the king of Assyria and the vast army with him, for there is a greater power with us than with him. With him is only the arm of flesh, but with us is the LORD our God to help us and to fight our battles." And the people gained confidence from what Hezekiah the king of Judah said. (2 Chronicles 32:6-8; see also 2 Chronicles 32:1-23)

Comparing resources can be deadly. Very likely we can always find someone who has out-maneuvered, out-resourced or out-foxed us. To remedy that kind of comparison, we need to be reminded of the wealth of resources we have. This was the genius

of Hezekiah's word of encouragement to his military officers and a
wise word to us as well.

What impact might Hezekiah's words have had on his officers as
they faced such difficult odds?

In what kinds of situations have you found that comparing yourself
to others produced fear? Why?

In what ways is our indwelling God greater than anything we will
face in this world?

Keep your eyes open this week for someone who is discouraged
because of comparing him- or herself to someone else. Remind that
person of God's indwelling resource, the Holy Spirit.

*God, use me this week to remind others that the one who is in them
is greater than the one who is in the world. And if I too need that
message, remind me of it through your Spirit or another encourager
like Hezekiah.*

DAY SIX

"Do Not Run Away": Jeremiah & Israel

*If you stay in this land, I will build you up and not tear you down; I will
plant you and not uproot you, for I am grieved over the disaster I have*

inflicted on you. Do not be afraid of the king of Babylon, whom you now fear . . . for I am with you and will save you and deliver you from his hands. I will show you compassion so that he will have compassion on you and restore you to your land.

However, if you say, "We will not stay in this land. . . . No, we will go and live in Egypt." . . . Then the sword you fear will overtake you there. (Jeremiah 42:10-16; see also Jeremiah 42:1-9)

M ost "Do not be afraid" accounts in the Bible result in people finding new strength to move forward. In this situation, however, Israel chooses not to heed God's encouragement. They are determined not to trust God but rather to scramble for their own solutions. That means running away from their situation.

What is significant about God's offer of deliverance coming on the brink of judgment?

Why is the pull so strong at times to trust in our own solutions rather than in God's deliverance?

Where do you feel you are determined to "fix a troubled situation" in your own way, ignoring God's way?

Lord, forgive me for those times that I have really messed up. Forgive me too for scrambling to fix it myself and refusing to correct wrongs the way you want me to. Remind me that refusing to return to you will only cause my fears to follow me wherever I go.

Small Group Study

When Fear Reigns & Motivation Wanes

Nehemiah was a master motivator. He managed to complete the rebuilding of the wall around Jerusalem in just fifty-two days. This in the midst of persistent, external opposition and internal discouragement! In fact, when it was complete, "all the surrounding nations were afraid and lost their self-confidence, because they realized that this work had been done with the help of our God" (Nehemiah 6:16). How did he do it? *Read Nehemiah 4.*

Faced with Opposition (vv. 1-3, 7-12)

1. Characterize the opposition levied against Nehemiah and the people rebuilding this wall.

What effect was it having on them?

2. Why would such opposition have such a draining effect?

3. When have you seen one of your own working groups similarly dismayed and discouraged? Describe that situation.

Fight for Your Brothers and Sisters (vv. 4-5, 13-14, 16-23)

4. What tools does Nehemiah use to motivate Israel to renew their efforts in the face of this opposition?

5. What keys to motivational leadership do you learn about from Nehemiah's example?

6. In what discouraging or fearful situation could you use these same motivational principles to encourage those with whom you work?

Enemies Are Thwarted (4:6, 15; 6:15-16)

7. What impact did Nehemiah's fearless leadership have on his own workers?

on those who were opposing them?

8. One of Nehemiah's gifts in this situation is weaving together a healthy balance between God's work and his workers. Why is such a balanced perspective critical but difficult to achieve?

9. Return to the challenging situation you mentioned before. What do you need to remember about God's resources?

about your own?

Pray that God will blend the two together into a strong, enduring fabric.

Weekly Wrap-Up

What range of fears are in this week's studies?

What principles have you learned about how to encourage someone not to be afraid?

What benefits resulted from these few words: "Do not be afraid"?

How did those words benefit you this past week?

Week Five

You Are Mine
Isaiah's Portrayal of God's
Commitment to His Suffering Servant

- -

DAY ONE

Streams in the Desert

The desert and the parched land will be glad;
*   the wilderness will rejoice and blossom.*
Like the crocus, it will burst into bloom,
*   it will rejoice greatly and shout for joy. . . .*

Strengthen the feeble hands,
*   steady the knees that give way;*
say to those with fearful hearts,
*   "Be strong, do not fear;*
your God will come," . . .

Gladness and joy will overtake them
*   and sorrow and sighing will flee away.*
(Isaiah 35:1, 3-4, 10; see also Isaiah 35:1-10)

How do you picture fear? Is it like a wilderness or desert? Is it knees knocking, hands and head drooping, and heart quivering?

Is it being lost on some deserted highway? This is how Isaiah sees Israel's fear on the eve of their exile. But he also sees hope for Israel with equally powerful images—images that speak comfort to those with fearful hearts. Let's look and consider.

How do the images in the first verses here convey hope on the eve of disaster?

Why would telling someone who is afraid, "God will come to you," dispel fear more deeply than telling them, "Your troubles will go away"?

What is meant in 35:10: "Gladness and joy will overtake them, and sorrow and sighing will flee away"?

When have you been aware of God's presence bringing beauty and life and strength to a dry and discouraging situation?

Almighty God, as you brought the Lord Jesus back to life from the dead, bring life and joy and gladness to my dry and dusty soul.

DAY TWO

Good News to Share

Comfort, comfort my people,
says your God.

Speak tenderly to Jerusalem,
  and proclaim to her
that her hard service has been completed,
  that her sin has been paid for. . . .

You who bring good tidings to Jerusalem,
  lift up your voice with a shout;
lift it up, do not be afraid;
  say to the towns of Judah,
  "Here is your God!"
(Isaiah 40:1-2, 9; see also Isaiah 40:1-31)

W e are often afraid to share the good news of Jesus with others, even our closest friends. Why is that? Well, in part it is because we know that to share good news we also at some point have to come to grips with the bad news. The good news is that God has come to us in Christ to forgive us and to care for us like a good shepherd (Isaiah 40:11). The bad news is that we continually ignore and rebel against God and do not humble ourselves to seek God's gift of forgiveness. In Isaiah 40 God encourages Isaiah not to be afraid to talk of God to others for the very reason that there is good news that is far greater than the bad news.

In Isaiah 1—39 Israel hears that they are on the eve of being exiled by God as punishment for ignoring and disobeying God. What good news about God's character is Isaiah urged to share in Isaiah 40?

Why is God so eager for Israel to know this good news of God's character on the eve of their exile?

Who have you been afraid to speak to regarding God's goodness? Why?

Heavenly Father, let me not hesitate to introduce others to who you really are when they are faced with bad news. Give me courage to speak boldly of God's coming to save.

DAY THREE

God Holds My Hand

So do not fear, for I am with you;
  do not be dismayed, for I am your God.
I will strengthen you and help you;
  I will uphold you with my righteous right hand.

For I am the LORD, your God,
  who takes hold of your right hand
and says to you, Do not fear,
  I will help you.

so that people may see and know,
  may consider and understand,
that the hand of the LORD has done this.
(Isaiah 41:10, 13, 20; see also Isaiah 41:1-20)

Picture the different ways people use their hands to help someone who is afraid: an arm around the shoulder, two hands holding another's hands firmly and compassionately, a hand outstretched to grasp the other's hand or shoulder, an open hand offering needed food or money, a hand leading another through darkness or danger, arms sweeping underneath someone to lift them up and carry them to safety, hands clapping to warn of danger, hands folded in prayer for another, hands on a head seeking God's blessing and anointing, a hand writing a note of encouragement. Hands are wonderful tools for dispelling fear!

How does Isaiah use the image of a hand to describe God's deep care for us?

Think of a situation today when you might need (or have already needed) God's hand to stay your fear. Imagine how God's hand might touch you today.

Think of someone you know whose heart is fearful. How can you reach out your hand to them today?

Precious Lord, take my hand,
Lead me on, help me stand;
I am tired, I am weak, I am worn;
Thru the storm, thru the night,
Lead me on to the light.
Take my hand, precious Lord, lead me home.
(Thomas A. Dorsey)

DAY FOUR

No Other Rock

Do not be afraid, O Jacob, my servant. . . .

For I will pour water on the thirsty land,
and streams on the dry ground;
I will pour out my Spirit on your offspring
and my blessing on your descendants.
Do not tremble, do not be afraid.

Did I not proclaim this and foretell it long ago?
You are my witnesses. Is there any God besides me?
No, there is no other Rock; I know not one.
All who make idols are nothing,
and the things they treasure are worthless.
(Isaiah 44:2-3, 8-9; see also Isaiah 44:1-11, 21-23)

When afraid, we all lean on someone or something to get us through our fears. The question is, how reliable is that source of comfort and strength? Sometimes the very things we rely on become our idols or addictions and only lead us to deeper fears.

How does Isaiah warn us about what we rely on to shelter us from fear?

In contrast, how does Isaiah encourage us to rely on the only true God for our salvation?

Why would our Creator be more reliable in dispelling fear and renewing our strength than anything he (or we) created?

How could our addiction to things that ease our anxieties actually deepen our fears rather than remove them?

To what extent do you turn to "idols" when you are afraid rather than to the one true God?

My Creator and Redeemer, let me drink in peace from your good hand, not from any broken cistern that could never satisfy.

DAY FIVE

Making Things Right

*Listen to me, you who pursue righteousness
and who seek the LORD.*

*The LORD will surely comfort Zion
and will look with compassion on all her ruins;
he will make her deserts like Eden.
her wastelands like the garden of the LORD.*

*The law will go out for me,
my justice will become a light to the nations.*

*My salvation will last forever,
my righteousness will never fail.*

Do not fear the reproach of men
  or be terrified by their insults.
(Isaiah 51:1, 3, 4, 6, 7; see also Isaiah 51:1-16)

It is not easy to pursue righteousness and to seek God, especially in an environment where people ridicule us for such efforts. Some of those threats or insults can be deeply troubling, even frightening. How can we serve God without fear in such settings? Isaiah struggled with this.

How does God comfort and encourage Isaiah (and Israel) not to be afraid of what others say and to pursue righteousness?

Why do insults and ridicule make us fearful when we are pursuing righteousness and justice?

How can God's reminders give you courage in those times?

When have you felt wronged recently?

How might God make it right for you?

As you have in days of old, protect me from feeling ashamed as I seek to follow you in a world that has turned its back on you (paraphrased from Isaiah 51:9).

DAY SIX

This Is Our Heritage

Sing, O barren woman,
you who never bore a child.

Do not be afraid; you will not suffer shame.
Do not fear disgrace; you will not be humiliated. . . .

For your Maker is your husband—
the LORD Almighty is his name—
the Holy One of Israel is your Redeemer;
he is called the God of all the earth.

O afflicted city, lashed by storms and not comforted,
I will build you with stones of turquoise,
your foundations with sapphires.
(Isaiah 54:1, 4-5, 11; see also Isaiah 54:1-17)

Visual images can illuminate concepts. No where is that more true than in this passage where Isaiah paints for us two pictures of fear and how God responds to each.

How do these two images, a barren woman and a beleaguered city, capture the character of fear?

How does knowing God as a loving spouse (v. 5) and as a rich developer (v. 10) help us to redefine the fearful situations in which we find ourselves?

Isaiah 54 ends with this strong affirmation: "This is the heritage of the servants of the LORD" (v. 17). How do these two images cause you to look forward more eagerly to your own inheritance from God?

O God, let me know that your love for me is more intimate than any of my deepest fears; and let me know that your plans for me are more spectacular than any of my shattered surroundings.

Small Group Study

God's Commitment to His People

Isaiah's words "Do not be afraid" are perhaps the most profound, the most uplifting and the most repeated over thousands of years of God's people facing fear's fury. One factor behind the strength of Isaiah's words is the depth of his understanding of God's own suffering servant who alone brings healing and salvation. Isaiah, perhaps more than any other prophet, declares the good news of the Messiah, the suffering servant, who is called Wonderful Counselor, Almighty God, Everlasting Father and Prince of Peace. *Read Isaiah 43:1-13.*

What Moves the Heart of God (v. 1)

1. According to verse 1, what motivates God to come to us in our fears?

2. What greater sense of worth does that awareness give you?

3. Which of these motivations behind God's care for us means the most to you right now? Why?

When You Pass Through the Waters (vv. 2-8)

4. What does God provide in the midst of our fears?

5. Why is it so important to know that God meets us in the midst of our fearful situations, not simply before or after?

How might that be strangely unsettling as well as comforting?

6. When have you wished that God would have "showed up earlier"—but with hindsight you know that he was there in the midst of it all?

What did God provide?

So That You May Know That I Am He (v. 10)

7. Why is God so eager for us to "know and believe" and "understand that I am he" (v. 10)?

8. What does it mean to be "witnesses" of God's presence as we face fearful situations?

9. How have you come to know God better as a result of your fear?

Have there been opportunities to share this with someone? Explain.

Weekly Wrap-Up

What images from your reading in Isaiah convey God's care for us when we are afraid?

What characteristics of God are highlighted?

Why do so many of these passages invite us to be "witnesses" to God's faithfulness in quieting our fears?

How could you give testimony to a way God has quieted your fears?

Who could you share this with?

Week Six

I Know My God Is for Me

The Psalmist's Struggles with Fear

- -

DAY ONE

The Lord Lifts Up My Head

O LORD, how many are my foes!
  How many rise up against me!
Many are saying of me,
  "God will not deliver him."

But you are a shield around me, O LORD;
  you bestow glory on me and lift up my head.
To the LORD I cry aloud,
  and he answers me from his holy hill.

I lie down and sleep;
  I wake again, because the LORD sustains me.
I will not fear the tens of thousands
  drawn up against me on every side.
(Psalm 3:1-6; see also Psalm 3:1-8)

How do we express our feelings of being overwhelmed and afraid? One way is to hang our heads down as if the whole weight of the world is crushing us. Another is to take our hand and signal how far up our face our troubles have risen. (Some draw the line at the throat, others at the nose, still others at the eyes—but we all fear that soon our troubles will cover our heads!) In any of these situations, what comfort it is to know that God shields us and "lifts up our heads."

In Psalm 3 what does God do for David that moves him to say he will not fear even if tens of thousands drawn up against him?

_____

In what ways does God "bestow glory on you" and "lift up your head" in times of trouble?

_____

In what situations does your head need lifting up today?

_____

O God, may you be for me today my shield and the lifter of my head so that I may think, see, hear and speak clearly and positively.

DAY TWO

The Lord Shepherds Me

The LORD is my shepherd, I shall not be in want.
  He makes me lie down in green pastures,
he leads me beside quiet waters,
  he restores my soul.

He guides me in paths of righteousness
 for his name's sake.
Even though I walk
 through the valley of the shadow of death,
I will fear no evil,
 for you are with me;
your rod and your staff,
 they comfort me.

You prepare a table before me
 in the presence of my enemies.
You anoint my head with oil;
 my cup overflows.
Surely goodness and love will follow me
 all the days of my life,
and I will dwell in the house of the LORD
 forever. (Psalm 23)

H as there been a more popular psalm for troubled times than Psalm 23? Let its powerful images speak to you again.

How would each of the tasks of a good shepherd mentioned help to wipe away your fear?

How would the shepherd's presence have such a comforting influence in your most fearful situations?

How would the treatment we see in the last set of verses further turn your fear into comfort?

May you, Lord, be my shepherd and banquet host today, especially when troubles surround me.

DAY THREE

The Lord Keeps Me Safe

The LORD is my light and my salvation—
  whom shall I fear?
The LORD is the stronghold of my life—
  of whom shall I be afraid?
When evil men advance against me
  to devour my flesh,
when my enemies and my foes attack me,
  they will stumble and fall.
Though an army besiege me,
  my heart will not fear;
though war break out against me,
  even then will I be confident.

One thing I ask of the LORD,
  this is what I seek:
that I may dwell in the house of the LORD
  all the days of my life,
to gaze upon the beauty of the LORD
  and to seek him in his temple.
For in the day of trouble
  he will keep me safe in his dwelling;
he will hide me in the shelter of his tabernacle
  and set me high upon a rock.
Then my head will be exalted
  above the enemies who surround me;
at his tabernacle will I sacrifice with shouts of joy;
  I will sing and make music to the LORD. . . .

I am still confident of this:
  I will see the goodness of the LORD
  in the land of the living.
Wait for the LORD;
  be strong and take heart
  and wait for the LORD.
(Psalm 27:1-6, 13-14; see also Psalm 27:1-14)

This image of the stronghold is realistic in two ways. First, it acknowledges the severity of the battle. There *is* much to fear. Second, it acknowledges the strength of a safe place. So there is even more to be confident about than to fear. Why not join King David in that stronghold!

What is it about God that allows King David to strongly declare his confidence even when surrounded by enemies?

_____

How would seeing the beauty of the Lord help David guard against fear?

_____

When do you feel surrounded by trouble or attacked?

_____

What aspect of God's beauty could you gaze upon today?

_____

Lord, you are beautiful beyond description. And I stand in awe of you. I offer you my praise.

DAY FOUR

The Lord Makes Me Glad

God is our refuge and strength,
  an ever-present help in trouble.
Therefore we will not fear, though the earth give way
  and the mountains fall into the heart of the sea,
though its waters roar and foam

and the mountains quake with their surging.

There is a river whose streams make glad the city of God,
the holy place where the Most High dwells.
God is within her, she will not fall;
God will help her at break of day. . . .

Be still, and know that I am God.
(Psalm 46:1-5, 10)

I still remember that fearful night. Several thieves had broken into our home while my wife and I were visiting neighbors. We returned to find our house stripped, two guests seriously injured, blood all over the living room and our two boys terrorized but safe. After helpful neighbors left late that night, we sat as a family around a tea table and read this psalm together—"God is our refuge and strength, an ever-present help in trouble." The fear was profound, but the refuge we found in God that night was even more profound.

Contrast how this psalm describes the overwhelming flood around us with the quiet stream within us.

What is the significance of God's help being described in verse 1 as "an ever-present help in trouble" and in verse 5: "God will help her at break of day"?

How does being still enable us to experience the quiet stream in the midst of the storm?

Dear Jesus, thank you that thieves cannot take you away from us!"
(Our six-year-old's prayer the night of the robbery.)

DAY FIVE

The Lord Redeems Me

Hear this, all you peoples;
listen, all who live in this world,
both low and high,
rich and poor alike:
My mouth will speak words of wisdom;
the utterance from my heart will give understanding.
I will turn my ear to a proverb;
with the harp I will expound my riddle:

Why should I fear when evil days come,
when wicked deceivers surround me—
those who trust in their wealth
and boast of their great riches? . . .

For all can see that wise men die;
the foolish and the senseless alike perish
and leave their wealth to others. . . .

But God will redeem my life from the grave;
he will surely take me to himself.
(Psalm 49:1-6, 10, 15; see also Psalm 49:1-20)

Think of all the times we are afraid because of money—either in the pursuit of it or in the loss of it. These anxious fears can strike both rich and poor alike. The Proverbs are full of wisdom about proper attitudes toward wealth, but here, tucked away in the Psalms, is a proverb addressing our fears about money. Listen and learn.

What fears can surround the accumulation, loss or lack of wealth?

How does understanding the two truths about death in the final two verses quiet any fears concerning wealth?

What financial fears do you currently struggle with?

Compare this psalm with Proverbs 30:7-9: "Two things I ask of you, O LORD; do not refuse me before I die; . . . give me neither poverty nor riches, but give me only my daily bread. Otherwise, I may have too much and disown you and say, 'Who is the LORD?' Or I may become poor and steal, and so dishonor the name of my God." What does it mean for the Lord to be your contentment?

Lord, help me in the midst of real financial fear to cultivate the wisdom and spirit of contentment.

DAY SIX

The Lord Keeps My Feet from Stumbling

Be merciful to me, O God, for men hotly pursue me;
  all day long they press their attack.
My slanderers pursue me all day long;
  many are attacking me in their pride.

When I am afraid,
  I will trust in you.
In God, whose word I praise,

in God I trust; I will not be afraid.
What can mortal man do to me? . . .

Record my lament;
list my tears on your scroll—
are they not in your record?

Then my enemies will turn back
when I call for help.
By this I will know that God is for me.
(Psalm 56:1-4, 8-9)

M any have found the psalms of David to be deeply reassuring in times of fear. One reason for this is that David himself was well acquainted with fear, especially during the years when he was hotly pursued by King Saul. For months at a time, David feared for his life and barely stayed one step ahead of Saul's hateful rages. David's psalms reflect both the depth of his fear and the depth of his trust in God.

When do you feel the kind of incessant pressure that King David describes in the first stanza?

Note how King David both praises God and petitions him. How can praise and prayer help to assure us that "God is for me"?

How can you cultivate the disciplines of praise and petition in the midst of your own fearful situations?

Are we weak and heavy laden,
  cumbered with a load of care?
Precious Savior, still our refuge:
  take it to the Lord in prayer!
Do thy friends despise, forsake thee;
Take it to the Lord in prayer;
  In his arms he'll take and shield thee;
Thou wilt find a solace there.
(Joseph M. Scriven)

Small Group Study

Resting in God's Shelter

Have you ever talked to yourself to try to quiet your own fears like "The Little Engine That Could" huffing and puffing up the hill and saying, "I think I can, I think I can"? Many times that monologue leans only on our own limited resources and dries up after a short time. But in Psalms we see another type of vulnerable yet trusting declaration that says, "I do not need to be afraid!" These psalms honestly admit to the overwhelming nature of fear and yet rejoice in the even more powerful cross current of God's amazing love. One example of that is Psalm 91: "He who dwells in the shelter of the Most High." *Read Psalm 91.*

No Fear Day or Night (vv. 1-8)

1. How extensive is the psalmist's declaration in verses 5-8?

2. How does it help you to know that the psalmist is aware of fear both morning and evening as well as in the heat of day and in the darkness of night?

3. What part of the day do you most dread? Why?

He Will Not Let Your Foot Be Moved! (vv. 9-13)

4. What images does the psalmist use to describe the help he draws from God?

5. Why would knowing these things about God help the psalmist to declare so strongly that fear "will not come near you" (v. 7)?

6. When have you witnessed God coming between you and the thing you feared?

He Who Rests in the Shadow of the Almighty (vv. 1-16)

7. How does the psalmist say we can appropriate this measure of confidence?

8. What is easy about that?

What is hard about it?

_____

9. How do you take time to "rest in the shadow of the Almighty"?

_____

10. Which, if any, of God's benefits mentioned in Psalm 91 have you come to enjoy?

Weekly Wrap-Up
_____

What psalm did you appreciate and why?

If you were to write your own psalm of deliverance from fear, what would you say? If you want help in stimulating ideas, complete the following and think of images that would capture both your fear and your trust in God.

The Lord is my _____

Even though _____

like_____

yet, I will not be afraid. For you are _____

I will _____

Read your psalms to one another in a time of worship.

Week Seven

Fearing God
The Heart of God's Covenant

- -

DAY ONE

Don't Forget What God Has Done for Us: Moses

Only be careful, and watch yourselves closely so that you do not forget the things your eyes have seen or let them slip from your heart as long as you live. Teach them to your children and to their children after them. Remember the day you stood before the LORD your God at Horeb, when he said to me, "Assemble the people before me to hear my words so that they may learn to revere me as long as they live in the land and may teach them to their children." (Deuteronomy 4:9-10)

Throughout this study we have been looking at the pervasive theme in the Bible of "Be not afraid." But an equally pervasive theme is "Learn to fear God." And the two are not unrelated. Learning to fear God is what "Be not afraid" is all about. And the One who has been coming to say repeatedly, "Fear not!" is also the One who is urging us to "Fear me!" This thought is embedded in God's covenant to us and is woven throughout the wisdom of Scripture.

What does God urge his people to do in these verses to help them remember his work and his ways?

As time goes on, why might it be easy for Israel (and us) to forget God's initial intentions for them (and us)?

Why is it important for us to remember the early days when we first committed ourselves to fear God and follow him?

What early memory do you have of wanting to fear and follow God?

How can you keep that memory alive?

"Praise the LORD, O my soul; all my inmost being, praise his holy name. . . . The Lord's love is with those who fear him, and his righteousness with their children's children" (Psalm 103:1, 17).

DAY TWO

The One Thing God Desires for Us: Moses

Now, O Israel, what does the LORD your God ask of you but to fear the LORD your God, to walk in all his ways, to love him, to serve the LORD your God with all your heart and with all your soul, and to observe the LORD's commands and decrees that I am giving you today for your own good? (Deuteronomy 10:12-13)

Oh, that their hearts would be inclined to fear me and keep all my commands always, so that it might go well with them and their children forever! (Deuteronomy 5:29)

Sometimes the command to fear God stirs in us uncomfortable thoughts or feelings: "Is God someone to be afraid of?" "Does he have our best interest at heart?" "Is what he expects of us more than we could ever do?" The children in C. S. Lewis' story *The Lion, the Witch, and the Wardrobe* struggled with these questions when faced with the prospect of meeting Aslan the lion.

> "Ooh!" said Susan. . . . "Is he—quite safe? I shall feel rather nervous about meeting a lion."
> "That you will, dearie, and no mistake," said Mrs. Beaver; "if there's anyone who can appear before Aslan without their knees knocking, they're either braver than most or else just silly."
> "Then he isn't safe?" said Lucy.
> "Safe?" said Mr. Beaver; ". . . Who said anything about safe? "Course he isn't safe, but he's good."

May we, like Lucy, learn how to fear God and trust him.

How do the statements following the phrase "to fear the LORD your God" help to explain what "fearing God" means?

How are these things "for our own good"?

What emotions come to your mind when you read the statement, "Oh, that their hearts would be inclined to fear me always"?

What difference does it make for you to know that God really longs for you to fear him?

In your own life when have you seen an example of fearing God being good for you?

Lord, give me a heart to long for the things you long for.

DAY THREE

Taking Time Out: Moses

Then Moses commanded them: "At the end of every seven years, in the year of canceling debts. . . . Assemble the people—men, women and children, and the aliens living in your towns—so they can listen and learn to fear the LORD your God and follow carefully all the words of this law. Their children, who do not know this law, must hear it and learn to fear the LORD your God as long as you live in the land you are crossing the Jordan to possess." (Deuteronomy 31:10-13)

Have you ever wondered why God set aside a sabbath rest every seven days, every seven years and every fifty years? Why did God himself rest on the seventh day after creating the whole universe? Is rest simply a luxury or is it absolutely essential?

How would obeying God's command to rest every seven days and every seventh year help us to learn how to fear God?

Why do we so easily let that kind of time get squeezed out of our schedules?

When could you take a retreat to listen to God and learn how he wants you to follow him?

Lord, I feel too busy to even consider resting—but maybe my life is too hectic because I have not rested. Show me how it can be done. May my trust in you compel me to rest and may my trust in you grow as I rest. And may I help others around me understand this life principle.

DAY FOUR

Fearing God Is the Beginning of Wisdom: Solomon

Let the wise listen and add to their learning,
and let the discerning get guidance. . . .

The fear of the LORD is the beginning of knowledge,
but fools despise wisdom and discipline.
(Proverbs 1:5, 7)

When discernment is needed in the midst of a most difficult situation, we often say, "I need the wisdom of Solomon to solve this problem!" Over centuries the wisdom of Solomon, captured in Proverbs, has proved to be invaluable counsel. Interestingly, Solomon was convinced that at the heart of wisdom is fearing God.

What might Solomon mean when he says, "The fear of the Lord is the beginning of knowledge"?

Why would this be so?

Why does Solomon describe the wise as teachable and fools as those who despise discipline?

Think of an area in which you are keenly interested or invested; how would fearing God enhance your wisdom and understanding in that area?

Lord, the next time I consider an issue, surprise me with what you might have to say about it, and let that begin to shape my own convictions.

DAY FIVE

Understanding the
Fear of the Lord: Solomon

My son, if you accept my words
  and store up my commands within you,
turning your ear to wisdom
  and applying your heart to understanding,
and if you call out for insight
  and cry aloud for understanding,
and if you look for it as for silver
  and search for it as for hidden treasure,
then you will understand the fear of the LORD
  and find the knowledge of God.
For the LORD gives wisdom,
  and from his mouth come knowledge and understanding.
(Proverbs 2:1-6)

What an invitation! In another section (Proverbs 4), Solomon reflects on the time he was a young boy and his father, David, helped him to understand how critical and valuable it was to fear God and embrace wisdom. Years later, Solomon now passes that counsel on to us.

How do the three sets of "if you . . ." lead us to understand the fear of the Lord?

Why is it also important to know that God gives wisdom to those who seek it?

What fear are you facing for which you earnestly need God's wisdom?

How could you apply your heart to understanding God's insight into that situation?

Lord, I am baffled about how to move forward in this difficult situation. Please give me wisdom. Thank you that you have promised to give it generously.

DAY SIX

Returning to God: Joel

Hear this you elders;
*   listen, all who live in the land.*
Has anything like this ever happened in your days? . . .

"Even now [before calamity comes]," declares the LORD,
*   "return to me with all your heart. . . ."*

Who knows? He may turn and have pity
and leave behind a blessing. . . .

Then the LORD will be jealous for his land
  and take pity on his people. . . .

Surely he has done great things.
  Be not afraid, O land;
  be glad and rejoice. . . .

"I will pour out my Spirit on all people."
(Joel 1:2; 2:12, 14, 18, 20-21, 28)

There are times that we should be afraid when we are not; and there are times we should not be afraid and we are. Oh that we would get it right! In the book of Joel God urges the people to rightly be afraid before calamity comes. They are to repent for all the injustice and unfaithfulness in the land. If in fact the people repent of their sin, God will not only forgive them but will generously give them the gift of his Spirit.

What various motivations to confess their sin does God give in this passage?

Why are we so nonchalant about sin, but then so afraid that God may not forgive us if we repent?

How would the Spirit cast out fear?

What can you do to begin to cultivate a right attitude toward sin?

How can your fear that God will not forgive you if you confess your sin be turned around?

Spirit of God, teach me to hate what you hate and to accept what you generously give. May I rightly fear your punishment but welcome your forgiveness.

Small Group Study

Learning to Fear God but Not to Be Afraid

At the heart of both Old and New Testaments is the theme of God's covenant. That covenant is clearly summarized in the book of Deuteronomy. And central to Deuteronomy is the Shema. At every Jewish sabbath and festival, the Shema ("Hear O Israel, the Lord our God, the Lord is One") is recited. This passage, more than any other, is at the heart of God's covenant to his people. Even Jesus himself refers to it when answering the question "what is the greatest commandment?" Three times in this chapter the Lord highlights the call "to fear him." May we never miss its importance. *Read Deuteronomy 6.*

This Covenant Given So That You May Fear Me (vv. 1-12)

1. How is Israel to go about ensuring that this covenant never gets lost?

2. What does it mean to "fear God"?

Why would that be central to how we view and heed the law?

3. Think of a time when fearing God has helped you or might help you obey him.

Fear Me Only (vv. 13-19)

4. What warnings does God give about our allegiances?

5. At Massah (Exodus 17) Israel bitterly complained about a shortage of water and provoked Moses to anger. Why is it so easy to blame God for things that go wrong?

What danger is there in doing that?

How is complaining different from crying out for help?

6. Think of a critical, even fearful, need you have. How could you choose to cry out to God for help rather than complain against God for not helping?

Answering Your Children's Tough Questions About Fearing God *(vv. 20-25)*

7. How should Israel go about answering their children's hard questions?

8. How would you explain the fear of God to your kids?

9. Take time to pray for your children or the children of a friend; pray especially for any fearful or confusing situations they may be facing.

Weekly Wrap-Up

From what different perspectives does God challenge us to fear him?

How do those perspectives convey the importance of fearing God?

Which of this week's passages did you find persuasive? comforting? troubling? Why or why not?

Week Eight

Your Savior Has Come

Enabling Us to Serve Him
Without Fear

- -

DAY ONE

You Have Found Favor with God:
Mary & Joseph

In the sixth month, God sent the angel Gabriel to Nazareth, a town in Galilee, to a virgin pledged to be married to a man named Joseph, a descendant of David. The virgin's name was Mary. The angel went to her and said, "Greetings, you who are highly favored! The Lord is with you."

Mary was greatly troubled at his words and wondered what kind of greeting this might be. But the angel said to her, "Do not be afraid, Mary, you have found favor with God. You will be with child and give birth to a son, and you are to give him the name Jesus. (Luke 1:26-31; see also Luke 1:32-38)

Because Joseph her husband was a righteous man and did not want to expose her to public disgrace, he had in mind to divorce her quietly.

But after he had considered this, an angel of the Lord appeared to him in a dream and said, "Joseph son of David, do not be afraid to take Mary home as your wife, because what is conceived in her is from the Holy Spirit. She will give birth to a son, and you are to give him the name Jesus, because he will save his people from their sins." (Matthew 1:19-21; see also Matthew 1:18-24)

Have you and a friend, colleague and or family member encoun-
tered very different fears as you face the same situation? Your
own fear is compounded by your fear for the other and wondering
how each of your fears could be addressed. This is what happens in
the Christmas story.

What different fears did Mary and Joseph have and how did the
angel address each one?

Watching the angel of the Lord handle this fearful and potentially
messy situation, what conclusions do you draw about how God
handles our unique fears?

Think of a situation in your family or at work where two of you
have different fears even though you are both in the same situation.

On the basis of this Christmas story, how are you encouraged to
respond to your own fear?

How are you encouraged to respond to the other person's fear?

*Emmanuel, you are God with us, and therefore you know and
understand the complexity of our situation. May you also show us
favor and gently lead us to a solution that we do not yet see.*

DAY TWO

I Bring You Good News
of Great Joy: The Shepherds

There were shepherds living out in the fields nearby, keeping watch over their flocks at night. An angel of the LORD appeared to them, and the glory of the LORD shone around them, and they were terrified. But the angel said to them, "Do not be afraid. I bring you good news of great joy that will be for all the people. Today in the town of David a Savior has been born to you; he is Christ the Lord. This will be a sign to you: You will find a baby wrapped in cloths and lying in a manger." (Luke 2:8-12; see also Luke 8:1-20)

What a spectacular birth announcement Jesus had! Just the shock of it must have been frightening—something totally beyond the shepherds' everyday routine. And they must have wondered why a wonderful announcement would come to such ordinary folk at such a strange time of night.

What grand intention did God have for this spectacular, awe-inspiring incident?

Why would God make his announcement to shepherds the way he did?

What good news of great joy does God have for you in this Christmas story?

Thank you, God, that you are always pointing people to Jesus, the Savior of the world. Would you please capture the attention of those who I would love to see meet this Savior, Christ the Lord, who was born for us. May I be as quick as the shepherds to go and tell others about this good news of great joy!

DAY THREE

From Now On You Will Fish for Men: Peter

When Simon Peter saw this [huge catch of fish], he fell at Jesus' knees and said, "Go away from me, Lord; I am a sinful man!" For he and all his companions were astonished at the catch of fish they had taken, and so were James and John, the sons of Zebedee, Simon's partners.

Then Jesus said to Simon, "Don't be afraid; from now on you will catch men." So they pulled their boats up on shore, left everything and followed him. (Luke 5:8-11; see also Luke 5:1-7)

Simon was a professional fisherman. He had several partners in business with him. They worked hard at what they did. They endured low spots in their business, like this time when they had fished all night and caught nothing. They also displayed generosity in lending their boat to Jesus from which he could speak to the crowds. And they were open, though somewhat skeptical, to trying new adventures. But something happened in the middle of all that which changed Peter's life forever. Here was Jesus, a carpenter who seemed to know more about fishing than Peter did!

What feelings did Peter's encounter with Jesus trigger?

What new sense of calling did Jesus give to Peter?

_____

How would Jesus' words to Peter help to diminish his fears?

_____

What sense of calling do you have for your vocation?

_____

What calling do you think Jesus has for you?

_____

How might a sense of calling diminish any fears that you may have, even any sense of unworthiness or sinfulness?

Lord Jesus, in your presence I am only too aware of my own short-comings. Help me to capture a true sense of calling that gives new meaning and worth to my life and work.

DAY FOUR

You Are Not Alone in the Storm: The Twelve Disciples

When evening came, the boat was in the middle of the lake, and he was alone on land. He saw the disciples straining at the oars, because the wind was against them. About the fourth watch of the night he went out to them, walking on the lake. He was about to pass by them, but when they saw him walking on the lake, they thought he was a ghost. They cried out, because they all saw him and were terrified.

Immediately he spoke to them and said, "Take courage! It is I. Don't be afraid." Then he climbed into the boat with them, and the wind died down. They were completely amazed, for they had not understood about the loaves; their hearts were hardened. (Mark 6:47-52; see also Mark 6:30-46)

Immediately prior to this frightening experience, Jesus had fed five thousand people on only five loaves and two fish. However, in the midst of this fearful storm the disciples were once again amazed as he calmed a raging sea, not understanding that if Jesus could do a miracle in one situation, he could do it in another.

Having seen Jesus feed over five thousand people, what confidence could the disciples have had to believe that Jesus would now help them in this terrifying situation?

Why would they see Jesus do miracles for people in one situation and then turn around and struggle with believing he could help them in this new crisis?

When have you seen God help someone else in a crisis but then wondered whether God would rescue you from your crisis?

O Lord, you who fed the hungry out of such a meager resource and you who calmed a raging sea, give me the faith to believe that you are able to come to me in my storm and bring peace, even though my crisis may be unique—different from any other I have seen you manage. Give me faith, especially when I feel I should know how to help myself.

DAY FIVE

You Are Eyewitnesses of His Majesty: Jesus' Inner Circle

Jesus took with him Peter, James and John the brother of James, and led them up a high mountain by themselves. There he was transfigured before them. His face shone like the sun, and his clothes became as white as the light. Just then there appeared before them Moses and Elijah, talking with Jesus. . . .

While [Peter] was still speaking, a bright cloud enveloped them, and a voice from the cloud said, "This is my Son, whom I love; with him I am well pleased. Listen to him!"

When the disciples heard this, they fell facedown to the ground, terrified. But Jesus came and touched them. "Get up," he said, "Don't be afraid." When they looked up they saw no one except Jesus.

As they were coming down the mountain, Jesus instructed them,"Don't tell anyone what you have seen, until the Son of Man has been raised from the dead." (Matthew 17:1-3, 5-9; see also Matthew 17:1-13)

Think of the awe of being one of the three who saw this spectacular view of Jesus. At first, this inner circle of Jesus' disciples saw him on a par with Moses and Elijah. As they witnessed the transfiguration, they were simply terrified by the full majesty and uniqueness of Jesus, even compared to Moses and Elijah.

Why would God cause this spectacular sight, yet then instruct the disciples "Don't be afraid"?

How can one develop a healthy view of who Jesus is—understanding his greatness without being terrified by it?

How do your prayers reflect that Jesus is more than a great teacher or prophet?

How do your prayers reflect an intimate closeness to this one who is full of majesty?

Thank you, Lord Jesus, that in our worship of you we can both fear you and be close to you.

DAY SIX

You Are Not Bothering the Teacher: Jairus

Now when Jesus returned, a crowd welcomed him, for they were all expecting him. Then a man named Jairus, a ruler of the synagogue, came and fell at Jesus' feet, pleading with him to come to his house because his only daughter, a girl of about twelve, was dying. . . .

Someone came from the house of Jairus, the synagogue ruler. "Your daughter is dead," he said. "Don't bother the teacher any more."

Hearing this, Jesus said to Jairus, "Don't be afraid; just believe, and she will be healed."

When he arrived at the house of Jairus, he did not let anyone go in with him except Peter, John and James, and the child's father and mother. Meanwhile, all the people were wailing and mourning for her. "Stop wailing," Jesus said, "She is not dead but asleep."

They laughed at him, knowing that she was dead. But he took her by the hand and said, "My child, get up!" Her spirit returned and at once she stood up. (Luke 8:40-42, 49-55)

The tension of this story is even more poignant when you realize that the daughter died when Jesus was interrupted by someone else who needed help. Can you imagine the tremendous emotional load on the father to hear his daughter had died while he was on his way for help? But now it is too late! Don't even bother Jesus anymore.

Describe your feelings when you know it is too late to do anything about something.

Why does Jesus encourage Jairus not to fear even at that moment?

What does that tell us about Jesus' concern and power?

What are you tempted to stop praying about because you don't think you can bother God with it anymore?

Teacher, am I hearing this right? Are you saying that it is never too late to bother you with a concern, even if it is too late to do anything about it? I can't believe that, but as you did with Jairus, encourage me to believe and not be afraid.

Small Group Study

Serving Jesus Without Fear

The biblical theme "Do not be afraid" is most prominent in the Christmas story. Fear grips every major character in this drama. In the Christmas story as told in Revelation 12, fear turns into fury when Jesus was born! But the greatest news of Christmas is this word: "Do not be afraid, because your Savior has come!" That news is captured best for us in the song that John the Baptist's father sang when his long-awaited son was born. *Read Luke 1:67-79.*

Rescue Is on Its Way! (vv. 67-75)

1. With the birth of Jesus, what wonderful news has broken through all the world's pain and suffering (vv. 68-71)?

2. What was God's motivation in sending him (vv. 72-75)?

3. How would this good news seek to dispel any fears we humans may have? For example, fears of loneliness? rejection? failure? insecurity? living in vain? seeing no way out?

4. Many have pointed out that some of the greatest anxiety and fear surface during the Christmas holidays. How have you noticed this with friends or in yourself?

Enabling Us to Serve Him Without Fear (vv. 74-75)

5. How does Jesus enable us to serve God without fear?

6. What is your biggest fear in living the Christian life?

What does Christ's coming into your life bring that will enable you to squelch that fear?

And You Will Prepare the Way for Him (vv. 76-79)

7. What role will John the Baptist play in preparing the way for Jesus to be welcomed?

What knowledge and insight about Jesus is John to present and explain? (Notice God's message in verse 77, God's motive in verse 78 and God's purpose in verse 79.)

8. Why is it important to take the time with our friends and family to help them understand why it is that Christ came, in order that they will be able to welcome him into their lives?

9. Think of a friend, colleague or family member with whom you could share the meaning of Christmas. How would you explain, for example, God's "tender mercy" or God's desire to "guide us into the path of peace"?

Weekly Wrap-Up

How do the four announcements of Jesus' coming that we have read reinforce the theme of "Be not afraid"?

How does Jesus' life help us not to be afraid?

Why do the angel of God and Jesus give so much attention to helping people understand clearly what Jesus was all about?

How do our fears often hinder that understanding?

What help did you have from friends or family to understand that Jesus came to save you?

Week Nine

"My Peace I Leave with You"

Jesus' Comforting Words During Passion Week

- -

DAY ONE

"See, Your King Is Coming"

The great crowd that had come for the Feast heard that Jesus was on his way to Jerusalem. They took palm branches and went out to meet him, shouting,
   "Hosanna!"
   "Blessed is he who comes in the name of the Lord!"
   "Blessed is the King of Israel!"
Jesus found a young donkey and sat upon it, as it is written,
   "Do not be afraid, O Daughter of Zion;
      see, your king is coming,
      seated on a donkey's colt." (John 12:12-15)

The atmosphere was electric! Jesus had just raised his friend Lazarus from the dead. And in the midst of that great excitement, crowds began celebrating Jesus' triumphal entry into Jerusalem. There was great anticipation of things to come—the best of which would be Jesus' becoming king. But drawing from Psalm 118 and Zechariah 9, John hints that sacrifice must come before success.

What fears might the crowds have on such a day of celebration?

When John juxtaposes the apparently conflicting images of "your king is coming" with "seated on a donkey's colt" (quoting Zechariah 9:9-12), how will this kind of servant leadership quiet Israel's deepest fears?

What fears of sacrifice have you had during a time of great success and anticipation?

How does Jesus' life of servant leadership encourage you to follow his example?

How does Jesus encourage you to have hope?

Lord Jesus, thank you for this reminder that in the midst of our successes we will face fear as well. May we, like you, humble ourselves as servants.

DAY TWO

"I Go to Prepare a Place for You"

"My children, I will be with you only a little longer. You will look for me, and just as I told the Jews, so I tell you now: Where I am going, you cannot come. . . .

"Do not let your hearts be troubled. Trust in God; trust also in me. In my Father's house are many rooms; if it were not so, I would have told you. I am going there to prepare a place for you. And if I go to prepare a place for you, I will come back and take you to be with me that you also may be where I am. You know the way to the place where I am going." (John 13:33; 14:1-4; see also John 13:31—14:14)

Some of our greatest flashes of fear are triggered by separation. And the deeper the intimacy enjoyed in the past, the stronger the struggle to embrace the future. The disciples were full of fearful questions when Jesus announced his departure. Yet Jesus understood their troubled hearts and assured them of a continued home together.

What kinds of fearful questions does separation trigger?

Why does it seem that the deeper the intimacy, the harder the questions?

What comfort does Jesus' promise of a heavenly home bring to such fearful questions?

What fear of separation do you struggle with the most these days? Sit down with Jesus and let him show you his plans for your heavenly home.

Lord Jesus, this separation really hurts, as it must have when you were separated from your Father. You now see the place He prepared for you and I thank you that you are willing to share that place with me.

DAY THREE

"I Have Overcome the World"

"You believe at last!" Jesus answered. "But a time is coming, and has come, when you will be scattered, each to his own home. You will leave me all alone. Yet I am not alone, for my Father is with me.
"I have told you these things, so that in me you may have peace. In this world you will have trouble. But take heart! I have overcome the world." (John 16:31-33; see also John 16:1-33)

The tension during the Last Supper must have been incredible. Already there were very serious threats and plans afoot to kill Jesus. The disciples would be a marked group. Plus, Jesus was deliberately taking time to explain to his disciples the necessity of his dying. All of this deeply troubled Jesus, and it deeply troubled the disciples.

What wisdom is there in Jesus telling the disciples they may only face more troubles when they already are feeling fearful?

What strength would the disciples find in the assertion that Jesus has overcome the world?

How would this confirm the truth that better than being told we will not face troubles is being given an inner strength to face those troubles?

Where do you most need that wisdom right now?

What overcoming and divine strength do you need most to conquer your fears?

Lord Jesus, as you assured your disciples, assure me that through your death and with the gift of your Spirit I may know a peace (John 16:33), a love (John 17:26) and a joy (John 15:11) that will renew my heart to carry on. Thank you.

DAY FOUR

"He Has Risen, Just As He Said"

The angel said to the women, "Do not be afraid, for I know that you are looking for Jesus, who was crucified. He is not here; he has risen, just as he said. Come and see the place where he lay. Then go quickly and tell his disciples: 'He has risen from the dead and is going ahead of you into Galilee. There you will see him.' Now I have told you."

So the women hurried away from the tomb, afraid yet filled with joy, and ran to tell his disciples. Suddenly Jesus met them. "Greetings," he said. They came to him, clasped his feet and worshiped him. Then Jesus said to them, "Do not be afraid. Go and tell my brothers to go to Galilee; there they will see me." (Matthew 28:5-10; see also Matthew 27:45—28:4)

Have you ever been afraid to believe something just because it was too wonderful to be true? You want it to be true. You would jump for joy if it were true. You hope that it is true. But because you cannot believe it is true, your fear that it is not true grips your heart and mind. Matthew, in telling this wonderful resurrection morning story, captures some of that for us when he describes these women as "afraid, yet filled with joy!"

What fears may these women be having as they are met and then commissioned by the angel?

When Jesus meets them again, just to say, "Do not be afraid," what extra comfort and assurance would that give these women?

Think of a promise of God's that if fulfilled would produce in you both fear and joy. What fear keeps you from believing that God can do that?

How can the example of the women encourage you not to fear?

Risen Christ, thrill me with the joyful reality of your resurrection and fill me with the immeasurable power of your new life in me.

DAY FIVE

"As the Father Has Sent Me, So Send I You"

On the evening of that first day of the week, when the disciples were together, with the doors locked for fear of the Jews, Jesus came and stood among them and said, "Peace be with you!" After he said this, he showed them his hands and side. The disciples were overjoyed when they saw the Lord.

Again Jesus said, "Peace be with you! As the Father has sent me, so I am sending you." And with that he breathed on them and said, "Receive the Holy Spirit." (John 20:19-22)

The disciples are caught. On the one hand, the tomb is empty and they are the prime suspects for stealing Jesus' body. On the other hand, the tomb is empty, Jesus is alive, and if the Pharisees wanted to kill Jesus because of Lazarus' resurrection, they are now the prime targets for being killed because of Jesus resurrection. The disciples' lives are in danger either way.

What does Jesus do to break into this fearful situation?

Why would Jesus' presence with them behind closed doors and his commissioning them to go out into the world as they had seen him do give them courage to follow their teacher's example, in spite of any danger?

In what ways do you feel completely trapped between two dangers even though something very good may be happening around you?

If Jesus suddenly showed up in your trapped situation and said these very same words, what new courage would that give you?

Indwelling Christ, thank you that you can walk through any locked-door situations in my life, calm my fear and commission me to carry on the same mission you had in the world.

DAY SIX

"Stop Doubting and Believe"

Now Thomas (called Didymus), one of the Twelve, was not with the disciples when Jesus came. So the other disciples told him, "We have seen the Lord!"

But he said to them, "Unless I see the nail marks in his hands and put my finger where the nails were, and put my hand into his side, I will not believe it."

A week later his disciples were in the house again, and Thomas was with them. Though the doors were locked, Jesus came and stood among them and said "Peace be with you!" Then he said to Thomas, "Put your finger here; see my hands. Reach out your hand and put it into my side. Stop doubting and believe."

Thomas said to him, "My Lord and my God!" (John 20:24-28; see also John 20:29-31)

The disciples are still afraid. And whether you are Thomas, who is full of doubts, or one of the other disciples who has already been convinced of the reality of Jesus' resurrection, you are hiding in fear behind locked doors.

What fear does doubt create?

What is the significance of Jesus' willingness to come back a second time for the disciples and particularly for Thomas?

Is there some area of your life in which you are struggling to believe? (Or do you know a friend or family member who is doubting?)

What encouragement can you claim from the risen Christ?

Risen Christ and Good Shepherd, thank you that are willing to go out of your way to help those who doubt, even if it is for just one person.

Small Group Study

"Let Not Your Heart Be Troubled"

When someone announces they are leaving, it so often feels like bad news because all the focus is on what will be lost. Imagine, if you will, Jesus' twelve disciples listening to Jesus in the Upper Room telling them that he is leaving. Think of all the things they will miss from their three years of constant companionship. To quiet their flood of fears, Jesus turns their focus from what they will lose to what they will gain. *Read John 14:16-19, 25-29; 16:19-23.*

I Will Send You Another Counselor (14:16-19)

1. On announcing that he will soon be leaving, how does Jesus reassure his disciples?

2. Jesus later says (16:7), "It is for your good that I am going away. Unless I go away, the Counselor will not come to you." What good does this Counselor bring?

3. When have you feared being abandoned or left alone?

My Peace I Leave with You (14:25-29)

4. What further reassurances does Jesus give his disciples?

5. In what ways does the peace Jesus gives differ from the peace the world gives?

6. When have you known the peace of Christ in your own life?

Your Grief Will Turn to Joy (16:19-24)

7. How does Jesus help the disciples to anticipate the feelings they will face in the days ahead?

8. What does it mean to say, "your grief will turn to joy?"

How do you see that as being true for the disciples (see Acts 2:46-47; 1 Peter 1:3-9)?

---

9. What grief do you long to see turn to joy?

How do Jesus' words in John 14—16 and Peter's words in 1 Peter 1 encourage you to anticipate that transformation?

Weekly Wrap-Up

What comfort does each of these seven Passion Week "Do not be afraid" statements bring?

What comfort do the cumulative thoughts bring?

Who could you share this comfort with?

Read Hebrews 2:17-18; 4:15-16. The writer of Hebrews says because Jesus himself suffered, he is able to sympathize with our weaknesses and to help others in their time of need. How do these verses in Hebrews reinforce Jesus' reassuring words during Passion Week?

Week Ten

A Peace You Cannot Fathom

Jesus & His Followers
Address Fears of Hardship & Hostility

DAY ONE

You Are More Important: Jesus

Therefore I tell you, do not worry about your life, what you will eat or drink; or about your body, what you will wear. Is not life more important than food, and the body more important than clothes? Look at the birds of the air; they do not sow or reap or store away in barns, and yet your heavenly Father feeds them. Are you not much more valuable than they? Who of you by worrying can add a single hour to his life?

And why do you worry about clothes? See how the lilies of the field grow. They do not labor or spin. Yet I tell you that not even Solomon in all his splendor was dressed like one of these. If that is how God clothes the grass of the field, which is here today and tomorrow is thrown into the fire, will he not much more clothe you, O you of little faith? So do not worry, saying, "What shall we eat?" or "What shall we drink?" or "What shall we wear?" For the pagans run after all these things, and your heavenly Father knows that you need them. But seek first his kingdom and his righteousness, and all these things will be given to you as well. Therefore, do not worry about tomorrow, for tomorrow will worry about itself. Each day has enough trouble of its own. (Matthew 6:25-34; see also Matthew 6:19-24)

Why worry? You may or may not say, "Well, for plenty of reasons." But in the Sermon on the Mount Jesus seeks to compel us with at least eight different reasons not to worry.

List as many reasons not to worry as you can identify here.

Which ones affect you the most? Why?

How much more important are you than the birds of the air, the flowers of the field, and the pagans and their pursuits?

How is this the key to dispelling fear and worry?

What is your greatest worry at work? at home? Consider again, how aware and invested God is in your concerns?

Heavenly Father, when I am tempted to worry about things, remind me of your care for your creation and how much more important I am than anything else in it.

DAY TWO

Nothing Can Separate Us
from Christ's Love: Paul

What, then, shall we say in response to this? If God is for us, who can be against us? He who did not spare his own Son, but gave him up for us all— how will he not also, along with him, graciously give us all things? . . .

Who shall separate us from the love of Christ? Shall trouble or hardship or persecution or famine or nakedness or danger or sword? . . .

No, in all these things we are more than conquerors through him who loved us. For I am convinced that neither death nor life, neither angels nor demons, neither the present nor the future, nor any powers, neither height nor depth, nor anything else in all creation, will be able to separate us from the love of God that is in Christ Jesus our Lord. (Romans 8:31-32, 35, 37-39; see also Romans 8:28-39)

W e can think of plenty of things that bear down on us and cause us to fear the worst. Paul's own list here illustrates that. What list would we make: fears we have already faced or those we are likely to face? What about those fears that are complete surprises and bring total devastation? News reports and phone calls are full of these kinds of frightening tragedies. What then shall we say in response to this?

Why is Paul convinced that God will stop at nothing to graciously give us whatever we need in the face of fear?

How do you feel when you read that absolutely nothing can separate us from God and from God's love?

What does it mean to be "more than conquerors"?

What has been the most difficult tragedy you have witnessed and who, if anybody, helped you to embrace a bit of the truth of this passage? How?

God, I cannot imagine what it felt like to see your only son maligned and murdered after sacrificing as much as he did for the helpless and the needy. Thank you that you went to the greatest length to show your love for your son by raising him from the dead. And I thank you that I have the same Father to show me that same love!

DAY THREE

A Peace That Guards
Your Heart & Mind: Paul

Rejoice in the Lord always. I will say it again: Rejoice! Let your gentleness be evident to all. The Lord is near. Do not be anxious about anything, but in everything, by prayer and petition, with thanksgiving, present your requests to God. And the peace of God, which transcends all understanding, will guard your hearts and minds in Christ Jesus.

Finally, brothers, whatever is true, whatever is noble, whatever is right, whatever is pure, whatever is lovely, whatever is admirable—if anything is excellent or praiseworthy—think about such things. Whatever you have learned or received or heard from me, or seen in me—put it into practice. And the God of peace will be with you. (Philippians 4:4-9)

Our minds can play funny games on us, and particularly in this area of fear. We can so easily think about the most unhelpful things when we are afraid. We often talk ourselves into things that are not true and we talk ourselves out of things that are true. We can think the worst about ourselves and about others. We can plot. We can suspect. We can hold grudges against others. We can panic and make rushed judgments and decisions. And in light of yesterday's study, one could see how the mind might very well be the devil's workshop. Here, Paul writes to a church he loves, urging them to ward off fear and anxiety by attending to the things they think about.

Notice all that Paul encourages us to do when we are anxious. How would this guard against fear and anxiety?

What does it mean when Paul says, "the peace of God . . . will guard your hearts and minds in Christ Jesus"?

How can you cultivate these thoughts this week to see your fear turn to a peace that passes understanding?

How could you help an anxious friend to do the same?

I praise you for being the God of peace. Guard my heart and mind moment by moment to conform to Christ so that I may be baffled by the peace you give.

DAY FOUR

The Reason for Hope: Peter

Who is going to harm you if you are eager to do good? But even if you should suffer for what is right, you are blessed. "Do not fear what they fear; Do not be frightened." But in your hearts set apart Christ as Lord. Always be prepared to give an answer to everyone who asks you to give the reason for the hope that you have. But do this with gentleness and respect. . . .

Dear friends, do not be surprised at the painful trial you are suffering, as though something strange were happening to you. But rejoice that you participate in the sufferings of Christ, so that you may be overjoyed when his glory is revealed. (1 Peter 3:13-15; 4:12-13)

Peter is well aware that Christians can find themselves in very difficult situations—often facing opposition and persecution when seeking to do good for others whether by service or witness. Peter urges us in such situations to look to Christ's own example for how best to respond to such hostility and hardship.

What counsel does Peter give to Christians facing opposition for their faith and good works?

What does Peter mean when he urges them not to be afraid in such situations but rather "to set apart Christ as Lord"?

What does he mean when he instructs them to "be prepared to give an answer . . . for the hope that you have . . . with gentleness and respect"?

What does he mean when he tells them that to rejoice in such situations we "participate in the sufferings of Christ"?

When has a non-Christian friend of yours asked you to explain why you believe or behave the way you do?

How did you answer?

Lord Jesus, let me count it a privilege when I end up suffering for doing good. First, let me know you are in control. Then, help me focus on the hope within me not the fear swirling around me. Finally, remind me of how you suffered for doing good.

DAY FIVE

Perfect Love Casts Out Fear: John

We know that we live in him and he in us, because he has given us his Spirit. And we have seen and testify that the Father has sent his Son to be the Savior of the world. If anyone acknowledges that Jesus is the Son of God, God lives in him and he in God. And so we know and rely on the love God has for us

God is love. Whoever lives in love lives in God, and God in him. In this way, love is made complete among us so that we will have confidence on the day of judgment, because in this world we are like him. There is no fear in love. But perfect love drives out fear, because fear has to do with punishment. The one who fears is not made perfect in love.

We love because he first loved us. (1 John 4:13-19; see also 1 John 4:7-12 and 20-21)

What is at the root of all of our fear? What is it, which if rooted out, would cause fear to flee? John, one of the inner circle of Jesus' disciples—the one Jesus was closest to and who is a leading elder of the early church—lends his insight into that question and puts us on a track that is very freeing.

What does this passage say about God's love?

When we know we are loved, how does that diminish fear?

John says in Christ we will not suffer ultimate punishment. What freedom does that give us?

Have you acknowledged Jesus as God's Son and gift of salvation for you? If so, what freedom from fear have you enjoyed because of that love relationship?

Love divine, all loves excelling,
Joy of heav'n to earth come down;
Fix in us thy humble dwelling;
All thy faithful mercies crown!
Jesus, Thou art all compassion;
Pure, unbounded love thou art;
Visit us with thy salvation;
enter ev'ry trembling heart.
(Charles Wesley)

DAY SIX

Once Dead but Now Alive: John

When I saw him, I fell at his feet as though dead. Then he placed his right hand on me and said: "Do not be afraid. I am the First and the Last. I am the Living One; I was dead, and behold I am alive forever and ever! And I hold the keys of death and Hades.

"Write, therefore, what you have seen, what is now and what will take place later." . . .

Then I saw a new heaven and a new earth. . . . I saw the Holy City, the new Jerusalem, coming down out of heaven from God, prepared as a bride beautifully dressed for her husband. And I heard a loud voice from the throne saying, "Now the dwelling of God is with men, and he will live with them. They will be his people, and God himself will be with them and be their God. He will wipe away every tear from their eyes. There will be no more death or mourning or crying or pain, for the old order of things has passed away." . . .

"I am making everything new!" (Revelation 1:17-19; 21:1-5; see also Revelation 1:9-16)

John now brings us to the end. He himself is exiled on the barren isle of Patmos. As he takes a quiet moment to worship God, Christ meets him and shows him a marvelous vision of things to come. As we read Revelation, we come full circle with our theme "Be not afraid." What was lost in the Garden is now recovered in the new city. The fear that entered our hearts with Adam is now gone forever in Christ!

How does the sight of the resurrected Christ instill fear?

How does it destroy fear?

How does the hope of a city without fear give us courage to live in our cities filled with fear?

What tears are you or a friend shedding?

What fears accompany those tears?

How can this promise of a time when there will be no more tears and no more fear encourage you?

Risen Christ, touch me as you touched John and wipe away my tears and fears with the assurance of my future with you.

Small Group Study

Cast All Your Anxieties on God

We come now to the end of *Be Not Afraid*. We have seen God come to people in fear over and over again and urge them not to fear because he is with them. Even in this past week's study we have seen New Testament teachers, who themselves have known suffering, encourage us to trust in God's unfailing love whenever we are afraid, anxious or troubled.

In this letter to Christians who are scattered all over Asia Minor and facing all kinds of trials and troubles, Peter invites us to "cast our anxiety" on God and gives three powerful reasons for doing so. May we learn to do this with all of our fears. *Read 1 Peter 5:6-11.*

Because He Cares for You (vv. 6-7)

1. What invitation does Peter give the Christians scattered throughout Asia Minor who are suffering all kinds of trials?

for what reasons?

2. In what ways does God's care for you compel or encourage you to cast all your anxieties on him?

3. What anxieties are you facing?

What would it mean for you to "cast" them on God?

Because Others Are Also Suffering Around the World (vv. 8-9)

4. What sobering challenges does Peter give us so that we may stand strong in the face of trials?

5. How does taking Satan seriously help us to stand strong?

6. How does remembering the suffering of others empower us to stand strong ourselves?

7. What examples of suffering around the world have motivated you to not be afraid in a difficult situation?

Because He Will Make You Strong (v. 10)

8. What assurance does Peter give these struggling Christians?

9. Why is this perspective on God's promise so helpful for fending off fear?

10. Thank God for how he has used this study to strengthen your group.

Weekly Wrap-Up

What reminders or pictures of God's love have you seen in this week's Bible studies?

How have this week's studies pointed to a future hope?

_____

How have we been invited to come to God with our fears every day?

In closing, sing "Amazing Grace." Consider together how prayer is key to handling our fears. Since this is the last study of Be Not Afraid, *perhaps you could share with each other how God has most encouraged you through this powerful theme in Scripture.*

How firm a foundation, ye saints of the Lord,
Is laid for your faith in His excellent Word!
What more can He say than to you He hath said,
To you who for refuge to Jesus have fled?

"Fear not, I am with thee; O be not dismayed,
For I am thy God, and will still give thee aid;
I'll strengthen thee, help thee, and cause thee to stand,
Upheld by My righteous, omnipotent hand.

"When through fiery trials thy pathway shall lie,
My grace, all sufficient, shall be thy supply:
The flame shall not hurt thee; I only design
Thy dross to consume and thy gold to refine.

"The soul that on Jesus hath leaned for repose
I will not, I will not desert to its foes;
That soul, though all hell should endeavor to shake,
I'll never, no, never, no, never for sake!"
(attributed variously to John Keene, John Kirkham and John Keith)